# THE AUTHENTIC WORKPLACE

How Authenticity is Creating
the Workplace of Tomorrow

**JEFFERY BUTLER**

# Copyright

Copyright © 2019 by Jeffery Butler

All rights reserved. No part of this publication may be reproduced, distributed, or transmitted in any form or by any means, including photocopying, recording, or other electronic or mechanical methods, without the prior written permission of the publisher, except in the case of brief quotations embodied in critical reviews and certain other noncommercial uses permitted by copyright law. For permission requests, write to the publisher, addressed "Attention: Permissions Coordinator," at jeff@jeffjbutler.com.

Ordering Information: Quantity sales. Special discounts are available on quantity purchases by corporations, associations, and others.

For details, contact the publisher at the address above.

Printed in the United States of America

ISBN-13:

# Dedication

*I dedicate this book to my parents and my father's grandparents who taught me the foundation of what I know about the workplace.*

# Acknowledgements

As with my first book, this book was a group effort. Thanks to Brian Comstock for prioritizing and roadmapping the process; if it wasn't for you, I probably would have started writing three books in addition to this one and not finished any of them.

To Marianna Guedez Forgiarini, for your endless help in the editing process. It was amazing to have your unexpected help. Astonishing how well-versed you are with English when it's your fourth language.

Thanks also to Rachael Krasner, a veteran editor of Jeff books. Thanks for all of your help in the editing process to ensure I don't sound crazy when I am putting my thoughts together. In addition, thanks to the many others who helped provide guidance in getting this book published.

# Contents

**AN AUTHENTIC INTRODUCTION** — 1
   A DIFFERENT BEGINNING — 3
   A BLOODLINE — 4
   RELATING TO WORKPLACE AUTHENTICITY — 6
   REAL ESTATE TO SILICON VALLEY STARTUP — 8
   EARLY TRAINING — 12
   WORKPLACE DIVERSITY — 13
   EMPLOYEE ENGAGEMENT — 14
   RECRUITMENT — 15
   EQUAL ABILITY EQUAL PAY — 16
   MISSION AND VALUES — 16
   MY INFORMAL EDUCATION — 17

**CHAPTER 1: A NEW WAY OF WORK** — 19
   AN INCREASING DESIRE FOR AUTHENTICITY — 22
   BACK TO REALITY — 25
   SELLING WITH AUTHENTICITY — 27
   AUTHENTIC RECRUITMENT — 30
   AUTHENTIC LEADERSHIP — 33
   AUTHENTIC MANAGEMENT — 38
   MOVING FORWARD — 41

**CHAPTER 2: DEFINING AUTHENTICITY AND ITS POWER** — 43
   BREAKING DOWN THE STANDARD — 45
   A BRIEF HISTORY OF AUTHENTICITY — 47
   MODERN ACCOUNTS ON AUTHENTICITY — 53
   HOLES IN THE DEFINITION OF AUTHENTICITY — 57
   HOW INAUTHENTICITY OCCURS — 63
   SPOTTING INAUTHENTICITY — 65
   THE POWER OF AUTHENTICITY — 67
   DEFINING AUTHENTICITY — 69

**CHAPTER 3: BECOMING AUTHENTIC** — 77
   BUILDING EMOTIONAL CONGRUENCE — 80

How Programming Develops - The Start
of Inauthenticity ..... 86
Congruence - Acting As Who One is ..... 89
Attunement - Utilizing Empathy ..... 92
Vulnerability- Expressing Emotion ..... 96
Staying on the Path of Authenticity ..... 99

**Chapter 4: Attracting Top Talent with Authenticity** ..... 101
The Shift to Authenticity ..... 104
Phase 1: Attention ..... 106
The Details Matter ..... 107
Creating a Strong Value Proposition ..... 111
Building Interest in An Authentic Way ..... 119
Stacking Interviews ..... 122
Creating an Unforgettable Experience Using Authenticity ..... 125
Commitment ..... 127

**Chapter 5: The Authentic Boss** ..... 133
The Most Optimal Team ..... 135
Align a Team ..... 144
Build a Strong Team Foundation ..... 150
Communication ..... 159
Managing Office Politics Through Authenticity ..... 166

**Chapter 6: Culture Driven Authentic Leadership** ..... 177
Transparency in Leadership ..... 180
Top Down vs Bottom Up ..... 185
Law of Connection ..... 189
Understanding the Complexity of Authentic Leadership ..... 193
Tips and Tools for Making a Culture More Transparent ..... 196

**Chapter 7: Moving Forward in the Authentic Workplace** ..... 201

**About the Author** ..... 221

# An Authentic Introduction

*"Just be yourself"*

I **CANNOT TELL YOU** how many articles, blog posts, slogans, tweets, IG shots, snaps, and books I have read that contained that quote. While the words ring with some truth, the phrase suggests a utopian impossibility. When taking a closer look at the text and really thinking about how people can actually be themselves, a counterpoint arises: how many people can actually be themselves every single minute of every single day? How many people can honestly say: *this is who I am* every day without ever deviating from "being themselves" due to request from another person? And no, I am not referring to the fitness Instagram models who post just about anything to get a few likes. I am talking about you and me, the everyday person, assuming you are not an Instagram model.

The honest answer is that there is no one who can be themselves all of the time.

Competing with this cynical view, when someone acts as themselves, for some very strange reason a magnetic aura emerges about them that makes them inexorably attractive and respectively real. Interestingly, very few of us, if any, will ever be able to achieve being ourselves consistently if we live in society. But, the word we associate with this heroic action is authenticity and by contrast, inauthentic as a moral crime.

A lot of mainstream media tosses this word around not giving much thought to it, assuming that as long as you are authentic in the world, the world will unfold for you, and most importantly, you can live a life without regrets. That being authentic is the pinnacle of a great character and should always be sought after. However, that is something you will learn is not true in this book.

What is authenticity, how is it useful, and how can it be beneficial to you? If you are like me, you probably never asked yourself these questions until you started seeing the word pop up through mainstream media in the recent political debates. However, before I dive into authenticity, what it is, its power and how to apply it, I recognize that everyone sees the world from a unique perspective and in this short book, much will be missed, or you may completely disagree with it.

The focus of this book revolves around authenticity and its relationship to the workplace. When relating the word authenticity to the workplace, most imagine a pushover boss who cares about giving out free hugs and spends most of their time managing people's fragile emotions by using sentimental feel-good language. Authenticity is not like that, so please don't think this book is like other books that assume that authenticity is a feel-good subject that results in everyone being happy. I don't blame you for thinking that with all of the different opinions of what authenticity really is; it's easy to get the concept convoluted with all of the ultra-positive *authentic* quotes out there in the world.

## A Different Beginning

When the word "expert" pop ups in your mind on the topic of management, recruitment, or leadership, you probably imagine either a Venture Capital-funded, blue blazer, thirtysomething startup founder infatuated with avocado sandwiches, or maybe a senior leader in a large corporation who believes dark green box suits from the 80s remain in style. Whatever you imagine, one of the biggest reasons why these personas are perceived as experts is because they have spent many hours in their fields or have done extraordinary things in their lives that others perceive as worthy. With that said, when you picked up this book you probably were under the impression that I was either a blue-blazered thirty-year-old who loves avocado sandwiches or a senior leader.

While I am not a senior leader, never raised millions in funding nor like avocado sandwiches (though I do like avocado in BLTs), I do have a pretty unique background. By the time I was 18, I had a MBA's-worth of in-field observation of management and leadership but I have never had formal training on either of the two. However, even at the young age of 27, I have helped fortune 1000 companies and addressed thousands of professionals across North America in the past few years on workplace topics.

In this introductory chapter, I would like to lay out my background in terms of how I see the world in terms of authenticity, where I have shaped my perspectives and insights in order for you to understand who I am and how the concept of authenticity entered my line of work. By taking this literary journey, you will learn about the different sides of authenticity, their relation to each other and your own life. Note, if you are looking for the application side of authenticity in the workplace, you would be better off skipping this chapter. However, it will give you a good reference point for where I am coming from in my viewpoints. With that said, to get a better understanding of who we are, we must understand where we come from.

## A Bloodline

In the 1960s, Jerry and Judy Butler in their early 20s and recently married, moved across the United States to Silicon Valley to start a new life. Jerry ended up working at Lockheed Martin and Judy was busing tables to help pay the bills. During that part of Silicon Valley history, silicon chips were just starting to be mass-produced, Intel had not been founded yet, and microwave technology had just become mainstream. Having an education from the Navy, Jerry already had a noticeably strong work ethic and found himself working in a respectable position that demanded a good amount of his time at Lockheed.

A short time after the two settled into the rhythm of their new jobs and began talking about the future they wanted to build for their children. As time passed, Jerry quickly rose through the company ranks receiving a promotion every other year. However, the company was not moving fast enough for Jerry's unbreakable work ethic and eventually he caught the entrepreneurial bug.

His nature was very driven, to the point where he didn't like the concept of only 40 hours over 5 days a week; 7 days and 80 hours a week was more his style. In the off hours, he began making financially aggressive moves that involved him using his savings to invest in different stock options. On the weekends, he would go to the stock floors, talk to stock brokers, cut deals and be on the hunt for new leads and information that could help him get the insider edge. At the time, there were no exchange-traded funds or computers to monitor the stock market, so he was able to hustle and make some fairly large deals in a short amount of time surmounting in the high tens of thousands of dollars of today. His field research involved visiting actual companies rather than listening to whatever Moneyweek was promoting.

After a few modest winnings in the stock market, he had enough money to make his first entrepreneurial move into real estate. At the time, he had an equivalent of $100k in his portfolio. With this money, he turned his focus toward investing in his first real estate property. After purchasing the property, he fixed it up and later sold it for a handsome profit. Wisely, instead of spending his cash profit on a new car or watch, he took the profits and made his next investment.

Over time, he began to make larger and larger investments using larger loans on each subsequent deal. All the while he was growing his real estate investment portfolio, he continued to work at Lockheed for supplemental income.

Eventually he earned enough to leave and when he turned in his notice, he founded a real estate company, which now in 2018, has a portfolio across Silicon Valley, Monterey, California and Las Vegas, Nevada.

It was the start of a bloodline.

## Relating to Workplace Authenticity

Here is where the story fits with the theme of this book. Jerry, my grandfather (if you haven't put the pieces together by our last name), had to hire a team, manage, and lead as his company grew. But he has a different workplace style than what I discuss in this book. Unlike the theme of this book, authenticity, he was extremely intense in the workplace. Now before people think of him as a negative figure, his style was very similar to notable leadership styles of Bill Gates and Steve Jobs. I am not a Steve Jobs fan. Sure, it is great what he did with the Apple legacy, but I just didn't agree with how he treated people. I don't advocate anyone to aspire to his style of leadership, but...it works.

They all had a style of being extremely demanding, avoiding sympathy and a whole bunch of other things that I don't want to include in this book. Leadership usually came through intimidation. For management, he would tell someone what to do and let them figure it out from there. If they couldn't figure it out, they were fired.

All what mattered was the objective. It didn't matter who was run over in the process. But unlike Steve Jobs, Jerry

# An Authentic Introduction

Butler didn't build for the glory to say he was changing the world, to have his face on *Forbes* magazine, or to show up and speak at conferences without a belt like it was no big deal. Jerry built just to build. He had an immensely difficult childhood that made it impossible for him to let off the gas in work that still keeps him going to this day. His level of intensity is unmatched. This intensity became clear to me a few years ago when he was in his 70s and he passed out in the airport on his weekly commute to Las Vegas. Keep in mind, he only had 30 percent of his heart function from past heart attacks, but he still made a weekly commute across states to meet with his team.

The crazy thing was that this approach of brutality worked, and it worked well. However, this came at the price of having difficulty with retention and occasionally engagement since it was based on fear. I bring this up because this rivals conventional thinking of the authentic approach as the only way to build a successful business — it is not.

Outside the workplace, Jerry was a very nice person, but as soon as work started, it was results or nothing. Any human resource employee would definitely have had him fired if he worked in a corporate company, then probably tweet about it. However, when someone can produce results from a team, it is very difficult to argue about the how, when, and the what when it is already taken care of. Later in this book, we will dive more into why technology is really advocating more authentic leadership styles than previous workplace generations.

The premise of this book is developing an argument that people in today's workplace look for an authentic approach in work relations more than what was happening previously in the Steve Jobs style.

Here is where the story gets fairly interesting and relevant to the book as the whole. While Jerry Butler used more of an authoritarian style, his son, James, who also became a Silicon Valley entrepreneur, was similar in some ways but entirely different in others. The big variable that set father and son apart? The emphasis of authenticity.

## Real Estate to Silicon Valley Startup

My father, James, grew up working for Jerry eventually went his own way in his late 20s. Even though he worked extremely close to my grandfather, being immensely influenced by his workplace style, my father did not manage and lead in the same way. My father shares a similar intensity, but he developed a strong ability to build relationships with his employees both inside and outside the workplace.

Like Jerry, James grew up initially investing in real estate. But with the changing times of Silicon Valley (this is taking place now in the 1980s), James knew technology was the direction to go. In the 1980s, just before I was born, my parents both had 9-5 jobs but had dreams of striking out on their own. My mother's parents were more academically focused; her father was a professor and her mother was a preschool teacher so a lot of that entrepreneurial drive to strike out was fueled by my father.

# An Authentic Introduction

Eventually, my parents saved up enough money to purchase their first rental home. Again, they continued working day jobs until, one day, my father decided to found a home inspection company: JMB Inspection, a glorious company that involved climbing under houses and in the most obscure places that no one else wanted to go. When selling a house, a house inspection is required for escrow, leaving a perfect business opportunity for my parents to fill. When I was very young, maybe 4, I remember my father's outfit that involved a grease-monkey blue suit and a mask like Bane from the Batman movies. It paid good money, but climbing under houses and looking for cracks in the foundation was no dream job.

In the mid-1990s, the tech revolution was well under way, so my parents both began taking programming classes at West Valley College — a junior college located in Saratoga, California. My mom, being the academic of the two, would breeze through classes while my father struggled through them even though he often taught my mother the material. Keep in mind, during this time my parents had several rental properties, a sole proprietorship inspection business and several children. Even with all of these obligations, they continued to educate themselves, knowing that the world of technology could transform their lives. Sometimes my father would bring me into college classes with him when I was 8 years old and I would bring in a book because the professors were lethally boring.

With the few classes and some leftover cash, my parents co-founded a hazard disclosure company that sold property data to real estate agents. They named the company

Terracheck. Being entrepreneurial, as they built the company they continued to apply classroom concepts to the business, including hiring the professor who was teaching the class to help code some things. His name was Raynor, and all I remember about him was that he was the tallest man I had ever seen at that time — 6'6". Here is where James started to build his first team and my paradigm of authenticity began to be shaped.

For recruiting, my parents in addition to posting job ads online, they also recruited the old-fashioned way through people they knew. They would talk about their idea and ask people if they wanted to be a part of the journey. Keep in mind too, that the company they were building was not the first of its kind and it wasn't destined to be the next Facebook or Google, so raising capital was out of the question. They built a company in a saturated space by being slightly better than their competitors. My parent's proudly state that, as a small company, they were the first company to start using spatial maps to represent the data on the industry disclosure reports. By the early 2000s, they had a company of 20 people with an office leased out in Los Gatos, California.

With his upbringing with Jerry, James learned that brutality was not the best route. By using a different approach in the workplace than Jerry keyed to authenticity and relationship-building, James reaped some very strong results. Take a look a look at some interesting stats regarding Terracheck.

1. My parents still have employees that worked with them in Terracheck working with them today. Yes,

people have actually worked with my parents for over a decade.

2. They **raised zero capital funding,** which means recruitment had to be either referral-based or compete against companies who had large recruiting budgets. Note social media was not available back then and Craigslist and Monster, the job ad company, were just coming into existence. Both parents had to focus strongly on retention because they didn't have the financial resources to keep hiring people consistently.

3. Neither parents had experience building a company team

4. Neither of my parent's had MBAs or prior tech experience aside from junior college classes.

5. My parents didn't buy one bean bag.

6. My parents' office wasn't located in **prime Silicon Valley (SF or Mountain View).**

7. They didn't paint icons represent company culture on the wall

Given all that, you would probably wonder how my parents were as successful as they were building a business with so little experience and not following a lot of common approaches to successful companies. The power behind what they did was less about what they did, but more *who* they were. One of those key elements was their ability to invoke authenticity in running the company.

## Early Training

My training in authenticity within management and leadership started slightly before Terracheck was founded. I was in middle school when I was first introduced to their office environment. It wasn't much of an office at first. They bought a property and were currently fixing it up, but also used it as an office. It was a small commercial building near Camden Avenue in San Jose, California. I remember meeting a few employees but never thinking much of the experience until I was in high school.

Once in high school, my parents relocated their office to Los Gatos, California. Their office now was conveniently located a bus ride away from my high school. On the weekdays, whenever I didn't have a sport to practice or a club to attend, I would take a bus ride to the 20-person software company and do homework in the conference room. Some days, I wouldn't do my homework and I would help around the office begrudgingly. Sometimes I helped by taking boxes to the recycling bin, wiring ethernet cables through rooms, setting up computers with the latest software, or my favorite, which involved creating a web crawling program that scraped data off of eBay. Without knowing it, I was becoming an active participant in their workplace environment.

During these periods, I was able to watch my parents manage and lead teams. At the time, I thought nothing of the fact that my parents owned and ran a tech company. The experience was quite normal to me. Having them in charge was normal because since I always did what my parents said and so did everyone else in the office- it felt like nothing new.

The more I was in the office, the more I started to build relationships with the employees there. The first person that comes to mind is Ryan, who loved basketball and would always take me down to the gym as a break to just practice. There was Gilbert, a software engineer who didn't talk much, but who used the money that they paid him to buy a 12-inch green spoiler that he put on his sports car. My parents still talk about how annoying that was to this day. There was Anesha who used to bring in her family recipes from India to share with her co-workers on Fridays. And there was Kris. She was famously known outside of the office for having pit bulls as rescue dogs. She was featured on Animal Planet regarding her efforts in search and rescue and had the honor of searching the NASA spacecraft crash in the early 2000s. Look her up on YouTube — Kris Crawford.

All of these workplace experiences began to develop my perspective and viewpoints about the working environment, introducing me to various controversial current-day hot topics.

## Workplace Diversity

Neither my parents or I hired with a goal off diversity; diversity just happened by hiring whoever was capable. When I now look at the large corporation with diversity officers, it seems a bit weird to me, not wrong, but different all the same. I never heard my parents trying to hire for a particular demographic, nor have I looked for a candidate that was of a particular background regarding an ethnic group. They just hired whoever could get the job done, though I understand why people push for it. It is really awesome to have equal representation of all ethnic groups in the workplace. Fun fact, my parent's and I have hired from every continent except Antarctica.

Culture was more of a celebrated thing in the workplace than a difference being pushed by a political agenda. We held potlucks where everyone would bring their favorite cultural meals. To help on the language front, my parents would go to Barnes and Noble and pick up books in the native languages of employees and ask them how to pronounce different things. In that sense, they were showing that they took an interest not only in who they were in the office, but also their cultural heritage. Very often, my father would pronounce things wrong or butcher a word, which got a few laughs.

## Employee Engagement

People love working for someone who they can relate to. One of the greatest things my parents did was learning as much as possible about their employees. I knew so much about the employees before ever meeting them because my parents would often talk about their employees and their personal lives at dinner. The key to their success was being able to develop a family environment in the workplace where people genuinely cared about each other.

On the surface, they seem like curious business owners, but underneath, they were building the foundation of a strong and healthy culture. Another way of understanding what they were doing was going from vertical to horizontal engagement. The process of having managers engage with people who report directly to them is called vertical engagement. Having employees engage with each other is horizontal engagement and that is where extremely strong company cultures are formed.

With diverse backgrounds and occupations, barriers are needed to be torn down and relationships formed; in other words, you need to build more horizontal engagement. In order to do this, my parents had monthly birthday competitions with personal trivia personal questions about the birthday person. The team who got the most questions right would get a gift card, go as a team to receive massages, or get their nails done. By employing these low-cost approaches, they were able to successful break down boundaries between departments and background to bring a more family feel to the workplace.

## Recruitment

On the surface, this seemed pretty straightforward: they would post a job ad, talk to a few friends and interview the candidate's with the best resumes. At the time in the 2000s, they would get some 300 applicants for a single job posting. They built a phone and in-person interview screening process for particular positions and went through each of the candidates one by one. They would often tell me stories about the way they hired. One story that I vividly remember was when they were interviewing someone for an accounting position who apparently had a criminal history having embezzled $50,000 from their previous employer. For the record, that person did not get the job.

## Equal Ability Equal Pay

On weekends, I would help my father with construction and we would work with a team of professional construction workers. It was here I started to learn my 7-days a week work ethic, but also how there were similar principles between the white-collar and the blue-collar working environments. While not all principles are the same, they are quite similar in many respects. And for those of you who are picturing just the men building a house, know that my mom would put on jeans and help out as well. No this wasn't gardening, this was actual outside work from digging trenches, pouring concrete, nailing in studs. My mom was there and there was no task she couldn't do. This is where my perspective of equal ability, equal pay comes into play. There is a lot of political turmoil regarding equal pay and gender. My viewpoint on this comes from growing up with a very strong mother who not only took names in the office but helped the boys outside with whatever was needed

## Mission and Values

Asking employees about the mission and values of a company and how they employed them in 360 reviews is probably the silliest thing I have seen. I will discuss this in the leadership chapter later, but the mission and values of the company are not something that are arbitrarily written on a wall, then everyone in the workplace somehow magically becomes that way. Mission and values of the company stem from culture, and culture is organically produced by the company. One big thing about working in my parents' company was the psychological safety that was present. The employees really felt that they could show their true selves in the workplace. This wasn't because my parents wrote safety as a company value, but rather it was from top down leadership and their ability to invoke such beliefs in themselves that it naturally trickled down.

## My Informal Education

With that said, a lot of people would assume that by receiving this special experience, I would have been building companies at 13, destined to be the next Elon Musk. This is definitely not true, and in fact, I never thought I would start a company until after I graduated college. What I learned in my household was not explicitly, "Jeff here is how you manage employees." It was more just watching, observing and subconsciously absorbing information not knowing it would be my career path in the future and form the pillars of my future company. From what I learned about authenticity growing up, I turned my focus to interviewing and researching the top companies in the world to see what they were doing differently that made them so effective, and then I discovered these companies all had something in common: this power called authenticity.

What I learned is that the most successful companies were starting to move away from the old style of authoritarian management to one that values authenticity, now addressing their employees and building teams through the elements of authenticity rather than intimidation. It is my goal with this book to help people see this trend and give them actionable things that they can apply to their lives and where they work to make it a better experience.

No one is forcing you to read this book or to be more authentic in your life. This book is for those who are looking for a better way of work, who are not satisfied with their current working environment and who want to change the stereotype of corporate America from an impersonal entity to one that is relatable, that is built by compassionate people. That is my sole purpose for writing this book.

And for you, I hope that you find this book helpful on your journey to make your work feel less like work. It might seem too good to be true that some of the greatest powers to make an unforgettable workplace come from our ability to be authentic with one another. That this power is not some technology for human resources, but rather a human ability that we all have, authenticity.

Chapter 1

# A New Way of Work

*"10 Million is all we need."*

During the company town hall meeting, a time where the executives give the greatest news for the entire company workforce to hear, the CEO of the Silicon Valley startup theatrically showcased the future projections of the company. With his large smile, unstoppable charisma, and heavy gestures, he explained where we were as a company, and what big plans we had for the future.

We were in the heart of San Francisco in the mid-2010s-SOMA area to be exact. This startup had big press releases to B-Class media outlets disclosing the greatest achievements that Silicon Valley was creating. It was one of those companies that attracted the college talent that could not to get into the Facebooks, LinkedIns or Snapchats. It was a second-tier startup, the ones that you don't hear about too much unless something bad happens.

I was one of the employees in the back of the room, arms either crossed watching the show or head down writing notes in a brown antique journal about the new business I was trying to start. Occasionally, I would look up at the presentation to ensure that if anyone was watching, it would look like I thought the quarterly town hall meeting was so remarkable that I was eagerly taking notes instead of reading the PowerPoint slides after the presentation, which no one ever did.

As the CEO continued, people were transfixed as the leader, who held the company's future, annual projections, dreams of its employees, and the payments of their bills in his hands, continued on dazzling and elaborating on what the bright future held before them.

What my coworkers didn't know about me at the time was that I was living the biggest humiliation that any startup founder could go through. You probably have heard about pursuing someone's financial dreams — building their own startup and becoming wealthy in doing so. Well, I pursued that dream when I was 25. I had a day job and a profitable software business that was a part of the family's holdings. However, I wanted to leave my day job, leave the family business and build a brand-new company that I was passionate about. With the little money I had, I left my day job, filed paperwork to sell my part of the family business, and started a new company. The next year, I successfully evaporated all of my savings.

When I mean evaporated, I mean everything. Down to the last rent payment and then having to put everything on credit cards in order to avoid being evicted. I never had credit card debt before, so this was a new sensation for me. That stuff piles up fast!

When you have no money and your business fails, you have two options: either move back in with your parents or go back to a 9-5. I choose the latter to avoid the humiliation of showing my parents that it was a bad idea, but hey, I had a dream.

"Here is the predicted quarterly projections and where we lined up."

The laser pointer pierced the wall just above the number '4' and '8' and to the right of a '5' & a '2' 48 and 52. We missed projections by about 4 points, but the CEO was happy with the steady progress that the startup was making. Everyone in the meeting seemed content with where things were going.

In the small leased out company room that probably housed 75 people, there was usually a Q&A section that followed the all-hands meeting. People would raise their hand to ask a question and someone would run over with the microphone while the CEO stood at the front of the room and listened.

'How are we doing on raising capital?'

I remember this like it was yesterday, the CEO rocked back onto his left foot and said, "We are great for a very, very, long time."

I didn't think much of that quote until two weeks later when the head of product brought the entire engineering team out to lunch. All 15 of us. She was paying, which was odd. As we all sat around the table, she mentioned she had an important announcement to make. As everyone stopped eating and looked out of respect at her sunglasses-covered face, she plainly said everyone in the company had been fired and today was the last day for everyone.

Why? Because last week we missed acquiring our Series C round of funding — All ten million dollars of it. The company was on its way to bankrupcy.

## An Increasing Desire for Authenticity

*'Innovation comes from a desire to make things better.'*

**- Innovation.Ca**

It is said that every innovation is motivated by a desire to protect a vulnerability, such as the psychological vulnerabilities of security and safety. With regard to security, one of our deepest needs for security comes from uncovering relevant information about our environment. Due to this necessity, we push for everything in our surroundings to conform to our need for security which we invariably apply to the workplace as well.

What I find so fascinating about this desire is that business experts such as Peter Drucker have stated that transparency is not a vital function of business. He states, "because the purpose of business is to create a customer, the business enterprise has two — and only two — basic functions: marketing and innovation." And yet, people are pushing for more than just marketing and innovation in order to appeal to their deep psychological needs instead of the vital functions for business survival — marketing and innovation.

Consequently, there are surplus functions being added to the corporate organism to appeal to people's vulnerabilities. Today, that organism now is needing to adapt to survive; by becoming a new entity that has authenticity as a vital organ in order to attract its main driving force — people; the drivers of the organism will also need to learn the power of employing companywide transparency to keep the organism alive.

When relating the desire for security to authenticity, to be authentic, as defined by Webster dictionary is to be "true and accurate." People often push for companies to be true and accurate to maintain a level of personal sanity in the realm of security. However, instead of being complacent, people have invented new ways of disclosing important information about modern companies to overcome this vulnerability beyond just company protocols.

One of the ways that people are making this a reality is by threatening companies with crowd-sourced reviews from internal employees to create worldwide corporate transparency. Glassdoor smartly discovered that people have an innate sense of altruism for helping complete strangers find their dream job. So they were able to acquire this information from the people who work internally at each company for free. Glassdoor curated this feedback and placed it on their website publicly to help future candidates understand the true authenticity of the jobs they are prospecting. The key to the success of this company was disclosing once-private information about internal culture, interviews, and even salaries. Because of the large amount of people going onto the website to view this internal information, Glassdoor began making profits by posting jobs to help recruiters. With that key insight, Glassdoor is now a leading company in the revolution of creating authentic workplaces.

All of these efforts are intended to increase transparency by attempting to answer the questions about how real the company is. The Society of Human Resources, in a survey[1] in 2015 focusing on Job Satisfaction and Engagement, identified "Management's communication of organization's goals and strategies (disclosing vital internal information to declare transparency)" as a key factor, assigning a 52% importance rating to the overall employee engagement strategy of a company. Adding to this importance, in the same survey, "Trust between employees and senior management" registered 64% in importance. With both trust and transparency through a manager's communication relating to authenticity, it can be explicitly seen that authenticity is becoming a vital part of the workplace.

---

1   https://www.shrm.org/hr-today/trends-and-forecasting/research-and-surveys/Pages/job-satisfaction-and-engagement-report-optimizing-organizational-culture-for-success.aspx

Workplace transparency is not the only aspect of the workplace that is involved in the increasing demands for an authenticity workplace, but rather, it's a small piece of a larger movement. There is a push for authenticity in transparency, authenticity in leadership, authenticity in marketing and authenticity in management. It appears in all different levels in companies each with its unique form and its own way to apply continuous pressure for corporations to change. Understanding these changes will place you in an excellent position to build the teams you desire, build the workplace you would like to work in, but most importantly, to understand where the world we spend so much of our lives in is headed and what it means for our future.

## Back To Reality

Being fired from the startup that screamed transparency was one of the most paradoxical things that ever happened in my career. To illustrate this paradox, the startup had an open floorplan, meaning there were no cubicle walls to hide mischief, there were transparent meeting rooms where anyone could watch meetings happening behind "closed doors," they even had consistent companywide meetings disclosing private financial information about the company's future to provide security, and occasional press releases letting the media know exactly what we were up to. Everything happening at that startup seemed to stem directly from an imaginary *Forbes* checklist on Top Ten Ways to Create a Transparent Workplace, inevitably leading employees to feel a strong sense of security and safety. And yet, despite everything being checked off the list, everyone was fired without notice — something broke down, but what was the cause?

Maybe I was too naive and drank the company's Kool Aid, thinking that everything was under control from a financial perspective. Many companies do surface-level things that could be found on major media outlet checklists to appear transparent and safe. However, in the startup's defense, it made perfect sense for a company to hide financial issues when they were close to going under, because if employees knew, most would have left, further increasing the chances of the company failing.

But why did I feel so betrayed? Why did this behavior just not seem right? Was it that I poured in hours of my time and consequently trusted the company, thinking that if I took care of my duties, they would be honest with me? It seems I had a strong expectation that the company would practice a level of honesty should things go astray — like a spouse being honest about an affair.

The Economist Article "The Disposable American - Layoffs and their Consequences,"[2] points out a trend that in corporate America brought to light by Drucker. "In the mid-1950s, management guru Peter Drucker emphasized that stable and secure employment helped build a highly motivated, committed workforce. The national job security consensus began to unravel in the 1970s; by the 1990s, it was gone." Implying we are at an all-time high for turnover and the expectation for job security is no longer a thing. With this

---

2   https://www.economist.com/media/globalexecutive/disposable_american_uchitelle_e_gA12_12567.pdf

recent shift, we still have a desire for security in a world without security. Sadly, this drive will probably be forever with us, given that security and safety is at the base of Maslow's human motivation hierarchy. Meaning that, we will be forever looking for a sense of transparency in a world without security.

Transparency is a small branch of the tree of authenticity, and while diving into the research, I noticed that the way that companies implemented authenticity took many forms, ranging from office layout to how someone leads a company. It can even be seen in the way that a company markets a product by appearing more genuine. All this suggests that authenticity is springing up everywhere in the corporate world in many different forms, leading to a new kind of workplace – *The Authentic Workplace.*

## Selling with Authenticity

*"Everything is changing"*

As cliché as that opening line is, the audience remained spellbound by his presence. He was the first of his kind — an entrepreneur celebrity, featured in various magazines with a social media following large enough to start a countrywide revolution. With such power, some called him a modern business prophet, while others called him one of the most annoying public figures since Kim Kardashian. With his frail 5'7" frame, he has enough energy to step in for the Energizer bunny commercials, known to work all day and night, only eating and using the bathroom once in the morning. Some even say he is one of the most interesting men alive, and his name, Gary Vaynerchuk.

Like him or not, Gary made history by being one of the first social media influencers to be brought on a major TV network show. Back in the early 2000s, Gary Vaynerchuk started a wine-tasting show where he video recorded himself talking about wine and uploaded to YouTube. Eventually, he attracted a large enough following ranging in the hundreds of thousands that ultimately got him on the Conan O'Brien show. Needless to stay, he knows a few things about social media, how to build a following, connect and, most importantly, sell.

He stated later in his keynote that, "to sell anything you need to have trust with who you are targeting" and later, 'that companies were going through a transformation that the consumer market is looking for a more human connection." He supported his premise by pointing out his "document vs create" methodology, a simple yet relatively new concept in the world of selling and building trust. He describes this method as instead of brainstorming and creating content, you document the experience. Essentially documenting what you are doing day-to-day and uploading the experience to social media — a much more real and uncensored authentic display of information — authenticity over professionalism.

This simple concept of "document vs create" can also be seen in reality TV where people are "having a reality experience" and demand a level of realism rather than a staged performance. However, the irony is, reality tv is heavily rehearsed to create the illusion of authenticity, but that is for a different time. An authentic veil over the pre-written show.

Contrasting with modern day selling, the 1970s sales movement found a lot of sales gurus popped up on the scene such as Tom Hopkins, one of his books being *How to Master the Art of Selling* to Brian Tracy's *The Psychology of Selling*. In these books, there was an emphasis on providing a customer with what they wanted, but also a push for quick, tactical solutions to sell customers, like the "door knob" or 'puppy dog" close, implying that the consumer was not smart enough to outmaneuver the manipulative salesman. Inevitably, the door-to-door salesman fell out of style as Marc Wayshak, an author and contributor to Hubspot, put it best in 2016: "these old-school techniques are simply regurgitated ideas that first appeared in the late 1800s and early 1900s. Even though they simply don't work anymore."

From there, selling started to shift to more of a warm soft approach from the titles: Daniel Pink's *To Sell is Human* to Amazon #2 best seller during 2018 Donald Miller's *Building a Story Brand*. In addition to books, plays such as *Death of a Salesman* have become nationwide hits. It might be less of the case that people enjoyed push selling, but rather, with technology we are able to avoid a lot of pushy salesmanship and leverage our authenticity to build a relationship that will help sell the commodity organically.

# Authentic Recruitment

In 2015, Aberdeen Group, a marketing intelligence company, pointed out that 73% of millennials, people born between 1981-2000, found their last job through a social network such as LinkedIn, Glassdoor, Twitter, etc. During the recruitment process, younger candidates evaluate companies through their brand on social media by looking at photos, engagement and also company reviews. The ability for a company to be authentic through these platforms can dramatically help them attract top talent to build a strong and healthy workplace.

The ability to recruit has gone from paper to digital. Vaynerchuk, mentioned in the previous section, leverages his digital media presence, not only for marketing his social media agency but also for recruitment. To illustrate this, 78% of millennials, according to eMarketer[3], are not appealed to by celebrity endorsements, so celebrities trying to promote a particular company won't work as much as someone who is credible and trustworthy. Vaynerchuk effectively deploys his message authentically on these platforms creating a strong pull for ideal candidates to join his firm. This is common among social media celebrities who are able to leverage digital media as a platform to garner attention, and surprisingly, to pull top talent away from the large corporate brands.

This technique to use social media as a recruiting tool symbolizes where the workplace is headed — stripping down

---

[3] https://www.marketingdive.com/news/study-78-of-millennials-arent-influenced-by-celebrity-endorsements/512170/

the corporate facade and appearing as a company that is relatable. In addition, I do think emails, phone calls, going to career fairs are all important techniques in the arsenal of recruitment. However, regardless of what part of the recruitment funnel, the point remains that being authentic is an invaluable tool in the world of recruitment.

Out of interest to this argument, if you are to Google "Zappos Recruitment Video" and look for their recruitment video released in 2012, you'll find an extremely good job of capturing an authentic workplace and connecting with viewers. A few things they did really well in the video are:

1. Showing actual people who worked in the company
2. Not using still-frame camera shots.
3. Using relatable humor
4. Having people in the film show their unique personalities.

Essentially, the video resonated with how most content is consumed today which is through social media — lower production and in a relatable form. The more you can appeal to the people evaluating the company, the better you will be able to connect.

Another approach that companies such as Space 150[4] are taking is using SnapChat to target future interns. Because that is where the candidates eyeballs are as there are 188

---

4   http://www.krtmarketing.com/blog/social-recruiting-10-companies/

million SnapChat users, according to Statisca.[5] Space 150 applied geofilters to send snaps to certain areas to get the attention of specific candidates and motivate them to apply to the firm. Interested candidates were asked to "Create a Snapchat story for one of our brands as if it were the year 2020." While on that platform, they needed to speak the language and be able to communicate in an authentic and personal way to attract the talent they were actively seeking.

Having a large corporate budget does not always mean that the company is doing a good job with recruitment. For instance, Google unfortunately did a very poor job of connecting with viewers in their recruitment video that had a VP of engineering introduce herself early in the video and then be awkwardly interrupted during the beginning part. Following a poor play at humor, the spot featured various interviews with people who worked at Google, all of which had an enormous amount of b-roll and editing that limited the viewer's ability to connect with any one individual person. Unfortunately, when this happens, it is much more difficult to connect to the audience. While the video was fantastic from a production standpoint, it stumbled on the following points:

1. High production
2. Cliché humor
3. Constant b-roll
4. Highly edited interviews.

---

5   https://www.statista.com/statistics/545967/snapchat-app-dau/

In summary here is where we are headed with recruitment.

| Past | Future |
|---|---|
| ■ Professional facade<br>■ High-quality production<br>■ Canned humor | ■ Authentic<br>■ Medium-quality production<br>■ Personal humor |

While we may have only touched on videos, we will unpack different parts of the recruiting process and demonstrate different ways of recruiting using the power of authenticity. Fortunately, recruiters are some of the most affable people and the strategies shared later on in the book will be able to leverage these personal talents. There are obstacles with sticking with company regulations and brand messaging, but sometimes it takes being a bit different to get attention from viewers. By using the techniques laid out in the later chapters, you will find easy-to-implement strategies to attract the right people to your workplace.

## Authentic Leadership

*"Bitcoin will never be a long-term success."*

These words were spoken during a press conference with some of the most well-known, yet ruthless media outlets all attentively listening. The media had been waiting for this moment for several hours in the hotel lobby, ready to ask the CEO a series of rapid-fire questions. All the questions that the journalists had brainstormed were already written out and all aimed at creating the most polarizing and attention-capturing headlines, because in a simplistic sense, what journalists live and die by — page views. If a journalist fails to get page views, they don't eat. As the words of Bitcoin's future escaped the speaker's mouth, the media gasped, realizing that they all heard the sound bite they were waiting hours to capture. As though it was performed ahead of time, synchronously, they all put their heads down and began writing. The loud and answer-hungry mob of journalists were now a silent monarch. Their work had been finished and there is no use for the CEO anymore.

If you were to look over one of the journalist shoulder's you would read:

"Jamie Dimon calls bitcoin a 'fraud.'"

The man who spoke of Bitcoin's future was unphased by the current circumstances. He knew what he did. He fed the wolves the meat they were craving at his expense. Every time Bitcoin does well, they will be asking him if he will want to retract that statement in order to expose his inaccurate forecast. More importantly, a mistake for a CEO in his position will always make headlines.

At the time, Bitcoin was exploding in popularity and each day millions of dollars were being invested in the new cybercurrency. There were investors who were already profiting from the new currency in the millions helping Bitcoin become a media stream sensation and the talk of the decade. To say that Bitcoin was going to be a failure was highly counterintuitive at the time.

That company, J.P. Morgan, and the CEO, Jamie Dimon.

Quantified Communication,[6] a data science research company that uses a combination of variables such as voice inflection, facial expressions, gesticulations to determine how well someone is communicating, analyzed Dimon's leadership abilities in 2017. That year, Dimon was rated by Quantified Communications to be the most authentic CEO in the group of *Fortune* 100 CEOs analyzed. On a scale of 0-100, Jamie was rated a 99, while the average score for other CEOS was 56 and the top 20 was at 88.

What really separated Dimon from the rest of the leaders was his ability to be authentic addressing both hostile and friendly audiences. From the linguistic analysis part of the study, Dimon was 41% more authentic than the rest of the CEOs when addressing controversial issues. As Quantified Communication suggests, "Inauthentic leaders struggle to engender trust and motivate employees, investors, or customers. But as we've seen with Dimon's success leading J.P. Morgan through years of turmoil, leaders who communicate authentically can inspire audiences to make extraordinary efforts on behalf of their organizations." What may be surprising to many readers is that Dimon does not agree with many mainstream perspectives ranging from political, controversial ideological, and financial policies and yet, people still trust him. This shows that one of the biggest shifts taking place in the workplace today is that people crave a unique perspective, and more importantly, someone who is willing to stand by their view.

---

6   https://www.quantifiedcommunications.com/blog/jamie-dimon-authentic-ceo-index

The startup founder in the beginning of this chapter, who fired of all his staff because of the startup missing its Series C funding, is a prime example of an inauthentic leader. For him to be an authentic leader, he would have needed to let his staff know ahead of time the severity of the situation. Behind the scenes, a large Venture Capitalist company was holding off on giving the startup the promised Series C capital for as long as possible, drying up all the startup's capital. When the CEO of the startup began demanding the large firm to hold up their end of the deal, the VC pulled out of the deal causing the startup to collapse. From there, the large firm acquired the startup for pennies, a shark move with flawless execution.

What is unfortunate is that the startup founder who makes a good decision will probably not be remembered for it. But if they make an inauthentic mistake, they will be stamped with that for the rest of their career. He lied and got caught making him a prime example of an inauthentic leader.

Another example regarding leadership is demonstrated in Mark Zuckerberg's behavior during a government lawsuit in 2018 related to the Facebook data privacy scandal. While the issue on the grand scale of things was not a large one, the media jumped all over it because of its symbolic relevance, that large corporate tech companies are using your data illegally and without your permission. In fact, even though Zuckerberg was not required to do so, he showed up in person to answer the hours of questions that Congress had for him which was authentic from a transparency standpoint. From these two risky yet authentic moves, he effectively saved both the company's and his own reputation in hopes of maintaining an authentic view of the Facebook brand.

In addition to those two authentic moves, in order to repair Facebook's tarnished reputation, a large marketing campaign was mounted regarding data control to repair their relationship with the general public. These ads can be found on billboards in public transportation areas and in online ads seeking to restore trust. During an interview between Adweek and Facebook's heading of marketing solutions, Carolyn Everson[7], who stated 'We've done ad campaigns. We've spent a significant amount of money here in the U.S. We're doing campaigns in the U.K., Australia, Germany, in a handful of markets. That's one positive thing. That's a step in the right direction to go out and admit fully our mistakes, take full accountability, and be transparent about what we're doing. So that definitely helped.' Point being, they were honest and authentic moving up to the plate in their campaign after the incident taking responsibility publicly on all fronts representing an authentic brand instead of hiding. A clear example of authenticity, however, how much this will repair their brand in the long run is hard to say.

Regardless of the type of leader, people are beginning to look for leaders who are able to stand their ground facing the social media mob through transparency and authentic perspectives. As Bill George, a Harvard Business School professor and CEO of Medtronic and his colleagues, conducted the largest leadership development study ever

---

7   https://www.adweek.com/digital/facebooks-carolyn-everson-rebuilding-trust-is-companys-total-focus/

undertaken on the matter to understand how leaders become and remain authentic. From interviewing over 125 business leaders from different racial, religious, national, and socioeconomic backgrounds the study[8] covered what makes an authentic leader in addition to finding the once tough and brutal leaders are going out of style, while a new collaborative leader is emerging that has more emotional attunement to their following. Later on in the book, we will break down Authentic Leadership into tangible actions that will enable you in your workplace to deploy the new levels of influence and authenticity.

## Authentic Management

*"I have cancer."*

That would probably be the last thing that you would expect a manager to say. All around, Matt's co-workers were silent and dumbfounded by their boss's heartbreaking news. Matt was recommended by a team at Google to take his team offsite to address some of the negative feedback his team provided in their feedback surveys. Project Aristotle, one of Google's most well-known research projects on team effectiveness, recommended that Matt specifically open up to his team about something in his life to create an atmosphere of psychological safety. Essentially, Matt was setting the tone using his news about cancer. What Matt did here was a classic example of authenticity by exposing vulnerability and setting the tone for psychological safety.

---

8   https://hbr.org/2007/02/discovering-your-authentic-leadership

However, I am not recommending that all managers should start revealing every vulnerability about their lives to build rapport. What I am recommending is the people look more into the power of being vulnerable in management because employees are more likely to open up and contribute great ideas to the working environment when they feel safe.

I told the story about Matt to a group of executives who at first glance all had the classic executive look — suits, ties and skeptical looks on their faces. Collectively, we discussed a few things happening in recruitment, management and the dramatic changes that have been occurring in the workplace. For example, the completely different strategies that are being used such as using social media as a megaphone and projecting an authentic voice. As conversation slowed down, I knew it was my time to leave. As I thanked the group and started to depart, an executive to my immediate left looked up and concluded, "I get it, basically, it is all about being authentic."

Project Oxygen, another research project done by Google focusing on the elements of the most successful managers, found that a manager's ability to coach is one of the most important elements to management. More specifically, a manager should act as a career coach by helping employees move forward in their career. With information being so abundantly available to employees and turnover so high, managers can no longer be that gatekeeper of knowledge. Instead, they can act as someone with experience under their belt to help the less-seasoned employees with decisions about their career paths.

But what does this have to do with authenticity? In order to have a relationship where someone is truly honest about where they want to go in their career, employees need to trust their superiors. Where does that trust come from? Authenticity. If a manager does not have this kind of relationship with an employee, they will fail to discover where their employee wants to go in their career, missing an invaluable opportunity to capture the intrinsic motivation.

Along with these interesting studies done by Google, Harvard Business Review in the article Management's Three Eras[9], written in 2014 by Rita McGath, states there were three different types of management styles in corporate history: execution, expertise and now today a new type of management is arising — empathy. As she reflects on the newest state, "This quest for empathy extends to customers, certainly, but also changes the nature of the employment contract, and the value proposition for new employees." While McGath would suggest empathy as the new management tier, I would agree with her, which is why in the next chapter I expand on how authenticity requires an element of empathy or attunement. With empathy now being central to management, it puts even more weight on the importance of authenticity.

Whether it's from Google or *Harvard Business Review*, there is a strong push for authenticity in management that is changing the way we work with one another. If a manager fails to implement these new methods, they will find their team will struggle with tenure. So then employees

---

[9] https://hbr.org/2014/07/managements-three-eras-a-brief-history

eventually leave for other managers who can deploy authentic relationships. If you ever plan to lead a team or have some project that involves interfacing with other individuals, I recommend checking out the Authentic Boss chapter.

## Moving Forward

There is a dramatic shift happening with regard to the importance of authenticity in the workplace. Whether that is leadership requiring a new level of transparency, management through the studies of psychological safety, or recruitment striving to build rapport with a candidate, nearly all parts of the workplace are being influenced by authenticity in some respect. However, if we are to leverage the power of authenticity effectively, we will need to first define authenticity precisely. Too many mainstream media sources stop at a definition that authenticity means "being true to yourself." However, as you dive deeper into the concept of authenticity, you will find a more complex and powerful meaning that will help in building an effective culture which you can also use in the workplace. In order to leverage the potential of authenticity, you have to understand that such power should be used wisely to reach its full potential.

CHAPTER 2

# Defining Authenticity and Its Power

*"I could stand in the middle of 5th Avenue and shoot somebody and I wouldn't lose voters."*

—**Donald Trump**

AT FIRST, I was very reluctant to include President Trump in this book because of his omnipresence in the news. But I think there is a very important point that should be taken seriously. That point is that you can be widely disliked, appear to be lying, yet still be perceived as authentic. Implying that, if someone knows how to deploy authentically effectively, they will still be liked without necessarily being politically or factually correct. While I am not advocating the use of authenticity as a manipulative tool, while it often is, I simply want to demonstrate the power of authenticity and how it can be used for good or evil.

In the year 2018, Donald Trump covers nearly every newspaper headline for his infamous quotes, and the American

Sociological Review[10] did some fascinating research on Donald Trump centering around his recent political election. The conclusion was that, even though he appears to lie or be factually inaccurate, he was perceived as extremely authentic. In further analysis, the study revealed several things:

- Trump's perceived authenticity (61.8% saw Trump as "highly authentic," and just 5.9% viewed him as "highly inauthentic.") was ranked higher than Hillary Clinton's which the researchers found that directly correlated to subsequent enthusiasm for him. Trump's authenticity was perceived to be higher than Clinton's.

- A significant number of Trump voters agreed that Trump did not literally mean the statement in his tweet. Similarly, Trump voters were more likely to view the tweet as "his way of challenging the elite establishment." Essentially, he said whatever was in the forefront of his mind.

- Trump voters were significantly more likely than Clinton voters to rate a vocalized or written statement as true: 68.8% saw the statement as highly false, compared to 95.5% of Clinton voters.

Given the Trump example, would it be fair to say that being authentic is a powerful tool that involves "just being yourself?" Well, no. A lot of Trump's statements were simply him saying whatever came to his mind, which often can lead to unexpected problems down the road. In this chapter, we will be getting fairly technical surrounding the meaning

---

10   http://journals.sagepub.com/doi/pdf/10.1177/0003122417749632

of authenticity along with revealing its power. You will uncover a lot of the modern-day myths and erroneous notions surrounding the pop culture character trait of "being authentic." While this chapter may seem lengthy, it makes sense because authenticity is the core foundation of this book. If we are not able to define it succinctly and accurately, the rest of the book will become flawed, erroneous and useless to the reader.

## Breaking Down The Standard

There have been thousands of books, poems and philosophical debates on what authenticity is in which the philosophical circles have analyzed the concept of authenticity extensively since ancient times. Let's look at several different definitions of the word authentic-

- Mike Robbins in his book *Be Yourself Everyone Else is Already Taken* — *"It's all about being yourself --understanding, owning, acknowledging, appreciating, and expressing all of who you are-- both the light and the dark."* Fair enough, this definition makes sense, discovering who you are whether that is good or bad and expressing that in the world. It sounds very noble and appreciative. Out of the three definitions here, Robbins has the most commonly accepted definition.

- Sue Fitzmaurice, states, "What it means to be authentic: to be more concerned with truth than opinions, to be sincere and not pretend, to be free from hypocrisy: 'walk your talk,' to know who you are and to be that person, to not fear others seeing your vulnerabilities." Understandable, being authentic will take a great deal of courage, but also implying that the definition that surrounds authenticity once again involves being yourself. Again, this author is focusing on authentic surrounding the resonance between who you are and how you act in the world.

- Charlie Chaplin (1889-1974) poetically concluded *"As I began to love myself. I found that anguish and emotional suffering are only warning signs that I was living my own truth. Today I know this is authenticity."* Here we find a bit different of a definition from the first two. Chaplin concluded that emotional suffering and anguish, essentially pain were the only determining factors that showed Chaplin that he was being true to himself, or rather being authentic. According to Chaplin, authenticity is a very painful attribute to act out in the world.

Here is where things get interesting. Traditionally, the Robbins and Fitzmaurice definitions surround the common thought for authenticity: "just be yourself, light or dark, and the rest will figure itself out." Usually, that means a "doing what feels right" attitude. However, Chaplin suggests the darkness behind authenticity regarding the emotional pain that can surround authenticity, which also simultaneously ties to how one respects oneself. Chaplin's definition adds perspective on self-love by taking authenticity one step deeper to reach the concept of emotional resonance. However, while these definitions seem to hold truth, there are still holes in these definitions and need a bit more analyzed to fully grasp what authenticity truly is.

We will first began by developing a stronger foundation of the word and be able to apply its potential in areas beyond what are written here in this book. In addition, the book is titled how Authenticity is becoming the workplace of tomorrow, so it would be worth considering how we came to the place where we now stand.

## A Brief History of Authenticity

The concept of *authenticity* has changed its semantic origin over time by several scholars who have been trying to define the complexity of its meaning. This continuous effort to define the word can be traced from to the Ancient Greek philosophers to the social theorists of our time. For that reason, the history of *authenticity* is as wide as the history of the philosophy. For the purpose of this book, I will provide a short look back into the most important part of history relating to *authenticity* to present day.

Perhaps one of the most influential figures of ancient times who reflected about the idea of authenticity was Socrates. For instance, many of his famous dictums seems to underline the everlasting questions: "know thyself" and "An unexamined life is not worth living," which according to Plato in its *Apology (38a5–6),* were the words spoken by the philosopher at his trial before he chose death rather than exile. For that reason, this statement has been perceived to stress the importance of understanding who we are by questioning and examining ourselves, even if that implies to die in that infinite search within.

For centuries, many other writers and philosophers reflected on the idea of what it is to be ourselves. However, the world had to wait almost 2,000 years after Socrates decided his fate to see the beginning of the modern conceptions of authenticity. In 1770, Jean-Jacques Rousseau, a Genevan philosopher and son of the Enlightenment, wrote his famous work *Confessions* which revolutionized the idea of authenticity. In this autobiographical book, the philosopher attempted to present a self-portrait by analyzing himself through the description of his own life. Indeed, Rousseau believed that he was embarking on an enterprise that was never attempted before, because *Confessions* was made to be an autobiography "in every way true by nature."

In this work, the philosopher argues that the direction towards life is guided by a force that comes from within. As a matter of fact, Rousseau, acting as the confessor, asks deep questions about self-reflection, introspection and inwardness, and opens his soul by telling the most unsavory and embarrassing experiences of his life. By doing this, the Genevan author infers about the idea of interiority in a different perspective, and realizes that the individual must distinguish central feelings, impulses and wishes from external forces and focus on the central motives of oneself. Upon this reflection, the author also claims that, if an individual acts on motives that are from the periphery of the self while ignoring the core of the self, they commit self-betrayal and produce at the same time the destruction of the self (Rousseau's The New Heloise (1997 [1761]). The philosopher also acknowledges that being ourselves is rather difficult, since we are surrounded by the public sphere which inhibits our ability to look inward. In more contemporary words, Rousseau perceives authenticity as a product of the natural self, whereas inauthenticity is behavior motivated by external influences.

In 1846, Soren Kierkegaard, who was not only influenced by Socrates perspective but who is widely considered the first existentialist philosopher, was able to provide another critical viewpoint on the idea of inauthenticity by comparing a certain social reality and a person's ability to act out of free will. On one hand, Kierkegaard judged aspects of his own social world, emphasizing that people were acting inauthentically by assuming a position as mere place-holders in the society. On the other hand, the philosopher rejects the idea that an individual should be seen as a substance with some essential characteristics, and proposes the idea of the self in more rational terms by saying "The self is a relation that relates itself to itself" (Kierkegaard 1980:13).

Furthermore, one of the main contributions to the idea of authenticity, by Kierkegaard, lies in the notion of subjectivity. According to Kierkegaard, subjectivity is the way that people are able to relate themselves to truths. For him, truth is not just a matter of discovering objective facts but, most importantly, is the idea of how one relates oneself to these "truths." Because, in an ethical perspective, an individual acts by following what they believe to be true. In this approach, Kierkegaard concludes that our truth is to be found in subjectivity, not in objectivity and by doing this we are "becoming what one is."(Howard V. and Edna H. Hong, "Subjectivity/Objectivity." *Søren Kierkegaard's Journals and Papers.*(Indiana University Press, 1975). In this case, Kierkegaard, known as a religious thinker, concluded that by following each person's subjective truth, they are in ultimate commitment to God by providing meaning outside of ourselves.

In spite of its religious belief, Kierkegaard point of view was an invaluable contribution to the first modern approaches about the idea of the self. However, the most familiar conception that we have upon the word "authenticity" itself belongs to the philosopher Martin Heidegger. Heidegger's conception of human existence (*Dasein,* "being-there") has its origin in Kierkegaard's ideas of the self. But, instead of thinking that the individual is an object among others, Heidegger believes that the self exists in a continuous relation between two ideas — what we are at any moment and what we can be in a temporary universe of possibilities. In this dichotomy, Heidegger points out that, over the course of our lives, we humans have our identities always unsettled; as projections into a future, without knowing exactly who we are.

Furthermore, Heidegger, in his famous work, *Being and Time* (1927), first coined the word *Authenticity* which is a neologism — Eigentlichkeit — created by the author and which more literally translate to "ownedness" or "being one's own." In other words, owning what one is or does. In his famous reflections, Heidegger expands upon the idea of authenticity in what it seems to be an evaluative-normative view of how humans behave. For that reason, inauthenticity is just the normal condition of everyday life, in which our own relations are influenced by others. However, the philosopher presents three behaviors of life: authentic, default (average), inauthentic. To understand this, for Heidegger, an authentic way of living life is "owned", an inauthentic way is "disowned," while the middle one is just how we live much of the time, in an "unowned" way. After the notorious fame of Heidegger's philosophy proposals, the word "authenticity" became known as the result of the early translations of *Being and Time* into English, and was lately adopted by other philosophers, who added their own ideas to its meaning.

Probably, the most important reflections about the meaning of Heidegger's new word — Authenticity — were written by the hands of the existentialist philosophers. Specially, Jean Paul Sartre and Simone de Beauvoir, each considering authenticity to add a deeper meaning to the first notions. This can be perceived by analyzing Sartre's most renowned work, which had an enormous influence on the intellectual sphere in the second half of the twentieth century, *Being and Nothingness: A Phenomenological Essay on Ontology* (1943.) In its work, Sartre describes the problem of human existence by breaking down our everyday lives and focusing on two specific ideas.

First, Sartre acknowledges that humans have "facticity"[that is what is given to us say through genetics] we must work with, such as our past, the body that we have and the social situation that constrains what we can do. In Sartre's work, the "in itself" does not have any specific attributes and is what we humans seem to share with other organisms in the universe. However, what makes the whole difference is that humans are able to question and choose who we should be. According to Sartre, this capacity to rethink ourselves by distancing ourselves from who we are allows us to organize what surrounds us into a different whole with meaning, which in Sartre words is the search for "transcendence."

Transcendence is the second specific element in Sartre's point of view and it's what ultimately allows humans to have the freedom to choose how they are going to interpret things, reconstituting ourselves through our own choices. In other words, for Sartre, although we are constrained by the facticity of our own situations, we have the power to decide our self-interpretations. However, the situation gets more complex because, according to the philosopher, humans are not only characterized by facticity and transcendence, but by the irreconcilable tension between the two elements — what Sartre called "Bad Faith" and the self-deception. For example, a person who believes that doesn't have courage as a "matter of fact" to exclude himself from transforming his own existence. The only way, according to Sartre, to survive this "Bad Faith" is to be authentic through finding a "self-recovery of being what was previously corrupted" (1943a:116).

Beauvoir, on the other hand, expands upon Sartre's description of the ambiguity of human existence in her work, *The Ethics of Ambiguity* (1948.) For her, the idea of freedom that Sartre relates as being authentic claims that necessarily the freedom of ourselves evolves into the freedom of all humans. Because, in Beauvoir's words, by achieving our own freedom we will infringe on the freedom to the others who will be able to find an unrestrained range of possibilities. Furthermore, Beauvoir continues with the idea that we humans are already trapped by social and specific situations that ask us for commitments of different sorts. This can be a tenuous and meaningless experience because we do not recognize an existential engagement to this occupation. However, according to Sartre and Beauvoir, an authentic self will be the one who decides, with its freedom, to act with decision toward what it's right in its context. In other words, the idea of authenticity is a continuous way of behaving with the idea of being true to ourselves.

## Modern Accounts on Authenticity

After the innovative works of these important philosophers in the twentieth century, philosophers, writers, social theorists and others added their own particular point of view to the word of *Authenticity*. In the 21th century, the modern concept was seen through a more negative light because of its moral implications. Consequently, over the last three decades, some authors has been taking a different approach, such as Charles Taylor (1989, 1991, 1995, 2007), Alessandro Ferrara (1993; 1998), Jacob Golomb (1995), Charles Guignon (2004, 2008) and Somogy Varga (2011). These authors have been working to reconstruct the meaning of authenticity by changing its original definition as *self-determining freedom* and keeping the idea of *transcendence*.

Taylor provides the theory that authenticity doesn't necessarily lead humans to ideas of self-indulgence because, according to the modern criticism, the critical point about authenticity is that the turn inward gets corrupted by the axiom of "being able to be free and do what we want without interference by others." The axiom itself is argued to be an extremely dangerous behavior that could break many moral codes (Taylor 1991:27). According to the author, self-determining freedom is not a necessary part of the definition of authenticity, because the process of constructing our identity is related to the idea of adopting a relationship to "the good," but is intrinsically connected to speaking the same language that our community does (Taylor 1989:34-35). According to Taylor's theory, we need the recognition of society in order to form our own identities or be authentic, and also need to engage with a common language of shared values to created collective realities.

Following with this idea, Alessandro Ferrara in his work, *Reflective Authenticity,* explores the relation between authenticity and validity. For the author, the world has to provide a universal validity that builds the normative ideal of authenticity that would serve as the core of the changing the definition of what well-being is. In other words, authenticity is characterized by a "self-congruency" of an individual, a collective or a symbolic identity (Ferrara 1998:70).

Golomb, on the other hand, provides an historical perspective on the genesis of the concept of authenticity and expands into both literary and philosophical sources. However, for the author, the most important aspect is the word's inherently social dimension. The author also takes a neutral position on the ethical value of its meaning, without having any special inclination to be authentic or inauthentic and perceiving both as part of the human beings.

Guignon also explores the philosophical roots of authenticity and its manifestations in the popular culture. Since Rousseau, he feels there has been a movement that believes that the dichotomy between being authentic and being inauthentic is the same as the notion of an inner child or an adult (2004:43). However, the author exposed that, according to the psychoanalytic conceptions of Freud and Jung, being an "inner child" is not as positive as the romantic concept suggests. Additionally, one of Guignon's main contributions on the idea of authenticity is the concept that we can understood being authentic as a dichotomy between a personal and a fundamentally social virtue at the same time. In other words, for Guignon, authenticity can be possible only in a society that is free and that possesses a solid core of established social values.

Finally, one of the last works in reconstructing the word authenticity, comes from Varga, who claims that the idea of authenticity "does not have to disappear but rather has to be reformulated." However, he also suggest that analyzing the original meaning of the word can provide some insight into the practice of the self in our own world. For Varga, we humans have to choose between "existential" possibilities that express who we are, and each one has a connection to the sense of necessity. In this choices, we are able not only able to articulate who we are, but by doing this, create our own reality. Nevertheless, we are not only able to discover who we are in our core, but we are actively constructing ourselves (Varga 2011a,b).

| Writer | Years | Definition of Authenticity |
|---|---|---|
| Socrates | 399 BC | Questioning and examining ourselves, even if that implies we die in that infinite search within |
| Rousseau | 1770 AD | As a product from the natural self, whereas inauthenticity is a result of external influences. |

| Writer | Years | Definition of Authenticity |
|---|---|---|
| Kierkegaard | 1846 AD | Following each person's subjective truth, they are in ultimate commitment to God by providing meaning outside of themselves. |
| Heidegger | 1927 AD | Self exists in a continuous relation between two ideas — what we are at any moment and what we can be in a temporary universe of possibilities. |
| Sartre | 1943 AD | Transcendence, the second specific idea in Sartre's point of view, is what ultimately allows humans to have the freedom to choose how they are going to interpret things, constituting ourselves through our own choices. |
| Beauvoir | 1948 AD | One who decides, with its freedom, to act with decision toward what is right in its context |
| Taylor | 1989 AD | We need the recognition of society in order to form our own identities or be authentic, and also need to engage with a common language of shared values to created collective realities. |
| Golumb | 1995 AD | Inherently social dimension. |
| Ferrara | 1998 AD | Authenticity is characterized by a "self-congruency" of an individual, a collective or a symbolic identity determined by society |
| Guignon | 2004 AD | Authentic and being inauthentic is the same as being an inner child or an adult |

| Writer | Years | Definition of Authenticity |
|--------|-------|---------------------------|
| Varga | 2011 AD | We humans have to choose between "existential" possibilities that we express as who we are, and each one has a connection to the sense of necessity. |

Through this small bit of history, we can see that defining authenticity is more complex that it may have originally seemed and goes beyond the simple idea of "being ourselves" as the first philosophers once believed. In this brief look back into history, we also were able to comprehend that the word "authenticity" not only was coined in the beginning of the twentieth century, but has suffered an extensive transformative process. Moreover, now we face the ethical implications that are behind its meaning and its impact on our society. Are we humans facing a new reality where we are looking only inward and forgetting our social limits? Or perhaps, we are approaching a better understanding of what it really means to be authentic in relation to our society?

# Holes in the Definition of Authenticity

For the section, we will keep the definition of authenticity as — "doing what feels true to you, and if you do so, you are being authentic." With authenticity, we make the assumption that we know who we are based on the emotional resonance of the action. If we feel good about what we do, that is authentic and, if it feels wrong, then it is inauthentic. In part of dissembling the current definition of authenticity, we will first analyze the concept of knowing "who you are" and why this is such a slippery slope if we leave this definition to emotional resonance.

## Hole One: Freudian Psychology

According to Freudian psychology, our subconscious mind can motivate the way we perceive what we think to be true. Meaning that what feels right for our actions might not be who we really are. Below is a story demonstrating the concept of false association in psychology:

Imagine a young girl that was brought up in a tough city run by a corrupt group of police officers. Each officer had a uniform of a blue coat, hat and pants. Whenever her parents were spotted by the police, the police officers would approach her parents and, without questioning them, begin to beat them. Each time this would happen, the young girl would run to a safe place and watch to avoid being beaten herself. During these terrible times, all she could see were the bluecoats above her parents inflicting pain on them while they lay helpless on the ground. Later in the girl's life, she was off in college far away from her corrupt hometown and faced a difficult decision. She was struggling in her course, so after hours she went to see the professor to ask a few questions about the subject matter that was covered in class. When the girl arrived at the professor's door, the professor was turned away from the door working on some paperwork and of course, he was wearing a blue coat, the same one that the officers used to wear as they beat down her parent's. Suddenly, the girl had a distinct feeling that this was not a safe place to visit, as professor would hurt her as the bluecoats had hurt her parents, so she abruptly left.

Was that action of leaving her professor truly authentic for the young girl, or was it influenced by memory from the past of something she was not consciously aware of? In this case, people would say her actions were inauthentic because what she felt was not true, mainly because the professor was not a police officer. Her brain alarmed her, prompting her to leave in order to avoid future pain.

Throughout our lives, we have situations resembling what this young girl went through to varying degrees, as our brains assemble defensive mechanisms to protect us in the future. In psychology, this is known as associationism, originally formulated by John Locke (1632-1704), that explains human intelligence, and holds that ideas that repeatedly appear in succession (such as darkness and sweetness of a banana) become associated so that any one of them can call to mind the others. In this case for the young girl, it was the blue coat association with immense amounts of pain. The reason why this invalidates the concept that being authentic is simply doing what feels right, since what feels right often results from subconscious protection mechanisms trying to help us avoid harm.

This complicates our definition of authenticity in two ways. One, it means what you feel might not always be who you are, and two, to become authentic, the journey would involve overcoming past trauma and terror. Meaning that whenever you are reflecting on whether or not you should do something based on how you feel, the way you feel is intertwined with past associations and also with who one is, both spoken in the form of an emotional tongue. The problem arises when emotion can be true but can also be based on erroneous associations. Unfortunately, without deep psychological analysis, it is nearly impossible to tell. One could be thinking they are acting authentically when simply trying to avoid past terror.

## Hole Two: Coexistence

In every culture and group, each individual person plays a unique role. Consequently, with their different levels of contributions, in some way or form they inevitably influence each other's existence. As John Stuart Mill's harm principle states, "Liberty is doing whatever it is you want in life as long as it does not harm other people or their property." However, this common definition of authenticity, of doing what you truly believe and is authentic, fails to acknowledge the presence of other people in the decision-making. If each person in a society did what was authentic for themselves without taking in consideration of others, two major problems arise.

The first involves a theory called Functionalism originally coined by Emile Durkheim. This theory interprets each part of society in terms of how it contributes to the stability of the whole society. Society is more than the sum of its parts; rather, each part of society is functional for the stability of the whole. Durkheim actually envisioned society as an organism and, just like within an organism, each component plays a necessary part, but none can function alone. As one experiences a crisis or fails, other parts must adapt to fill the void in some way. Taking into account the theory of functionalism, applying its use can dismantle authenticity in a simple thought experiment.

Hypothetically, say there were two individuals, both acting in terms of being authentic with their main objective being survival. They can only eat animals and two people must be present when they kill each animal. Authentically, they both want to eat the whole animal. However, in order for both to survive, each person would have to give up some personal liberty in order to work together to slay the animal, and not be authentic while eating half of the animal rather than the whole animal. If one continuously eats the whole animal without ever sharing, the other person dies, and the selfish person will inevitably die too because there is only one person left. Hence, giving up personal liberty to reach to a greater outcome for the group is mandatory when one lives within a non-anarchical society.

Secondly and more on a humorous note, let's look at authenticity as the ability to act in a way that is most true to the individual and compare that with this definition from the Stanford Encyclopedia of Philosophy: "Egocentricity, deceitfulness, impulsivity, a lack of empathy, and a lack of guilt and remorse. Particularly relevant for assessments of moral responsibility is the psychopath's inability to care for others and for the rules of morality." If someone was to consistently act in a way of being authentic to themselves, they could subsequently act in a way that an impulsive and psychopathic, according to this paper. Hence, if you are truly authentic in doing whatever feels right for you without consideration for others, you inevitably display psychopathic traits.

From this section, we covered some holes in mainstream's definition of authenticity, and realize that, if one were to act authentic, all of the time, it that would not work in a societal structure where one needs to compromise absolute personal freedom. In addition, acting from a place from only considering your own needs is a form of psychopathology and self-centeredness.

## Hole Three: The Noble Savage

Among of the problems that surround the concept of authenticity, the most controversial one is the argument of the Noble Savage, which holds that humans are born perfect, meaning that simply changing child-rearing will make us all morally sound individuals. It also suggests that humans inevitably become corrupted by society, which is the source of evil. However, Steven Pinker in his book, *The Blank Slate*, points out numerous weakness in the Noble Savage argument. Relating this to authenticity, it is often said that if you have a feeling of doing the right thing, as in acting in an authentic way, it *should* be the right thing to do. However, since there are inconsistencies in the Noble Savage argument, what may feel like the right thing to do may not be the right thing after all because humans may not be at their foundation perfect beings.

My viewpoint on the Noble Savage concept is that it should not be used as a premise for authenticity when the Noble Savage argument itself is unstable. With this said, something that feels right may not be the most moral thing to do, hence being authentic does not mean that someone is acting from a place of moral perfection. Because being authentic is *not* correlated with doing "good" things, since people at their core might not be "good" people.

## How Inauthenticity Occurs

Inauthenticity very often is seen in a negative light, but being inauthentic is mandatory for human existence. Indeed, the basis for inauthenticity is one's ability to act in a way that is not in alignment with core desires. However, as you will learn, being inauthentic is often a very smart thing to do.

The first avenue where inauthenticity occurs is in the first hole discussed in the previous section — Freudian Psychology. A common example is distorting a response to a question to avoid causing someone pain. This phenomenon often occurs in situations of cooperation where each party is in a confidential situation where each needs to act a way of inauthenticity for mutual benefit.

In 2012, I was first introduced to a game in a political science class called Prisoner's Dilemma where each game is a true demonstration of inauthentic behavior. The game played in the class was a derivative of Prisoner's Dilemma to represent the complexities behind international politics. Each person in the classroom had a red and black card. If everyone put a black card down, the entire class got +200 points for each person. If someone put a red card down, that individual person got +100 points and the rest of the class got none. If multiple people put a red card down, each person who put a red card down received +100 points. The goal of the game was to have the most points after 20 rounds.

Naive as I am, I never put a red card down. However, I was surprised to find over half the class put the red card down consistently. Note, there is no prize for winning the game in class, it was just the pride of saying you won. After 10 rounds, a student in the back of the classroom was probably going through the same questioning of humanity as I was, but unlike myself, she decided to take action. Reaching into her bag, she started to pull out different packs of gum and items that had actual value in the *real world*. She then began to plead with the class for that just one round of the game that everyone put down the black card. In exchange, everyone would get these packs of gum and, after class, would buy each student their favorite candy. Lastly, she said that this game was symbolic of humanity and we need to make a change. The result, a good part of the class still put the red card down. We all didn't get candy.

I don't think I will ever forget that class, not because I lost miserably, but I learned that, in order to survive, inauthenticity was a better long-term strategy for the group, while an authentic strategy worked better for the individual. More succinctly, behaving inauthentically would mean putting down the black card with everyone profiting by avoiding selfishness at the expense of the group. Authenticity on the other hand, would mean putting down the red card and profiting while the rest lose. This example shows that we are placed in structures that test our ability to act authentically. If we are not able to execute this in the classroom without stakes, how can it be executed on the world stage with all the stakes imaginable?

Inauthenticity also occurs to avoid social repercussions. In the second hole of the definition of authenticity — Coexistence — people in society are required to act in harmony with one another. This results in people needing to act in ways that might not always be in alignment with who they are and what they want. For instance, let's consider someone who is very conscientious about their body weight. It would be authentic for them to notice other people's weight who did not match their expectations. However, most people who exhibit this particular preference, usually don't outright tell those people directly that they are overweight to their faces. If someone would exercise that kind of behavior, they would be perceived as someone who does not understand social dynamics and be accused of narcissism. In order to avoid this kind of social situation, we see that being inauthentic is a better long-term strategy in this case.

Overall, inauthenticity is a trait that is intrinsic to humans and it is not necessarily a bad thing. Our utopian ideal that we should be authentic all of the time violates our need to live in a society, but also shines a negative light on being conscientious of others which will lead to being inauthentic. Concluding, if we were to live in a society where everyone lived by authenticity according to the mainstream definition, we would end up in a world of anarchy filled with psychopaths and narcissists unaware of other people's emotions.

## Spotting Inauthenticity

Spotting inauthenticity happens when there is a discrepancy between one's words and actions. A person says they are going to do 'y', but their body says they want to do 'x'. Very often, we cannot tell consciously why someone acts authentically rather than inauthentically, unless it is very prominent. Examples such as a person showing numerous lying cues, such as looking around the room and becoming extremely nervous are easy to spot.

Subconsciously, we have an internal radar for this. Some neuroscientists attribute this to mirror neurons, which that are believed to assist the brain with learning and empathizing. The French-German scientist, Christian Keysers, describes mirror neurons as "multimodal association neurons that increase their activity during the execution of certain actions and while hearing or seeing corresponding actions being performed by others. Neurons responding to the sound or sight of some actions, but only to the execution of different actions, are not mirror neurons." Mirror neurons are also thought to play a role in understanding someone's intentions and being able to anticipate why they are doing something. This is where it touches upon authenticity. If there is a gap between one's intentions and actions, the person watching notices it and the inauthenticity alarm goes off.

The neuroscience community is divided about whether mirror neurons have an influence over empathy, with some arguing that mirror neurons are actually quite underplayed. V.S. Ramachandran of the UC Berkeley Greater Good Psychology Research Center believes that mirror neurons could be the foundation blocks of psychology, as he stated "mirror neurons will do for psychology what DNA did for biology." However, today we may not be able to pinpoint exactly what elements of the brain do what, but we do know more about the psychology perspective on how someone is perceived in terms of their communication.

This art of nonverbal communication is often referred to as the 55/38/7 Rule. This rule holds that when you are listening to someone talk, the amount that you like them breaks down with 7% of the impact due to Verbal Liking, 38% to Tonal Liking and 55% to Facial Liking. The formula was arrived at by Albert Mehrabian and Susan Ferris in 1967 explain the weight that a listener places on elements of a communication *only* when a speaker is talking about their feelings and attitudes. They combined the results of two separate studies to reach this conclusion. The stat that usually surprises people is that viewers only give about a weight of 7% to liking the content when someone is expressing their feelings.

If you can imagine then, when someone is describing an emotional experience to another person, the recipient is not paying attending to the words nearly as much as they are paying attention to the non-verbal communication — body language and tonality. Hence, if the non-verbal communication is out of alignment with the content, a flag is set off in the viewer's mind that the person speaking is being inauthentic.

## The Power of Authenticity

After seeing the abundant examples of how the workplace is shifting to a world of authenticity, telling you the power of such an attribute could be self-evident. By leveraging the power of authenticity, the wielder becomes adept at building trust with whoever they are addressing. As we saw earlier in this chapter, trust outweighs truth, meaning that people in a way become strongly persuaded by someone who they perceive as authentic. This ability has been often used by politicians around the world, such as Trump with his ability to project his message in an "authentic" way. People begin to look past the politically incorrect statements and see the intention behind the actions. However, whether you plan to use authenticity for good or evil is up to you, you will find that, the better you are able to invoke attributes of authenticity, effectiveness will rise in all areas of the workplace — leadership, management and recruitment. Authenticity is the key to trust.

Jordan Peterson PhD, a *New York Times* Bestselling author and clinical psychologist, stated that "Deception [The ability for someone to do one thing while thought to do another] is one of the worst experiences someone can go through." On that note, authenticity acts as an insurance policy where people begin to trust you and feel that they understand who you are more clearly, so they believe you won't deceive them. They essentially pull down their guards leaving themselves in a vulnerable position. In a way, authenticity works as an antidote for deception because if someone is authentic, then the person listening will feel that they can trust the speaker to avoid trickery. This could account for why we are so attuned to non-verbal communication when analyzing someone according to the 55/38/7 rule that was discussed earlier.

Here are some of the benefits are leveraging authenticity in the workplace:

- Employees are more likely to open up emotionally with a manager who promotes psychological safety.

- People are more likely to follow an authentic leader than one they do not trust.
- Improve retention of employees.
- Creating companywide transparency.
- People trust you more.
- Recruiting more effectively both on an initial basis but also from a long-term perspective.
- People listen to you more.

While that does not cover all of the benefits, the biggest thing that authenticity brings is trust in the workplace. In a world that is in constant change and turnover, having someone you can trust is like a lighthouse for a lost ship in the immensity of ocean. It gives someone direction to follow and someone to depend on in the waves of life.

## Defining Authenticity

Now that we have thoroughly explored authenticity, we will need to define it succinctly, so we can have a solid foundation moving in to the later chapters. I originally derived this definition by breaking apart the current definition, then juxtaposing that to what people perceive as authentic. In this book, I propose that there are dimensions of authenticity: attunement, congruence and vulnerability.

## Attunement to Others

When communicating, there needs to be an overlap between the recipient's reality and your own. Often, when people convey being authentic it involves someone saying whatever comes to their mind. However, this will not be in attunement with the audience's reality. Essentially, attunement is that touch of empathy that can really make a difference in communicating with someone. It is the difference between being obnoxious or stating the elephant in the room that everyone wants to hear. An easy way to picture attunement is in the diagram below: the person speaking is the projector and the recipient has their own reality within that circle. The middle is the authentic zone.

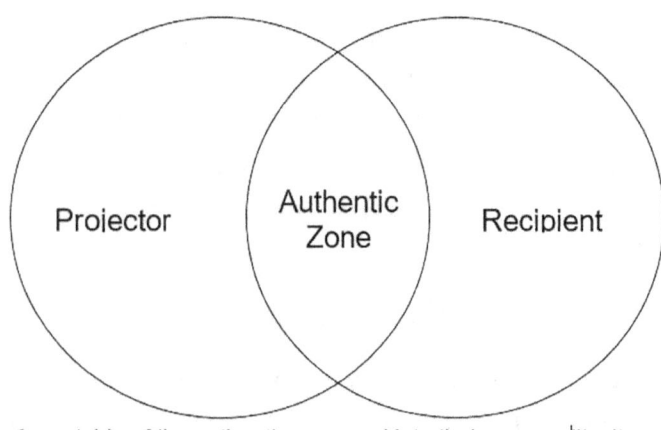

If one goes too far outside of the authentic zone and into their own reality, its means that they are either being too vulnerable or too out of touch. For example, when you initially meet someone, there is a certain range of topics that you can discuss based on the environment and current situation. As you get to know that person better, the inner circle expands, meaning that you and the other person can talk about more things. Eventually, you will be able to address very vulnerable issues that are appropriate and authentic. However, imagine if you shared this really personal information with the person when you first met them. They will probably be freaked out and the relationship will be ruined from the beginning. Hence, there needs to be a sense of empathy, or in other words, I refer to it as attunement to the other person's reality. Attunement is essentially understanding the reality sphere of the other person.

As time goes on, you will be able to share more personal information with that person consequently opening up the authentic zone. This effectively addresses the psychopathic concept of just being yourself when being authentic. People have a personal range that where they feel comfortable sharing private information and if the other person oversteps this boundary, they come off as obnoxious or not in tune with the other person's reality.

## Emotional Congruence

Remember the 55/38/7 rule that people spend a lot less time on whether or not they like you based off of the content that you are saying? It's only about 7% of the content and the rest is body language? Well this dimension handles that effectively. This section is also where the standard definition about "being yourself" falls into. In this dimension, he truthfulness of what you say does not matter, all that matters is whether you are emotionally congruent with what you are saying. As you probably noticed earlier in the book and reading through various "being authentic" quotes on Pinterest, a lot of the quotes are about speaking the truth. Here is the catch, it is the truth to that person. How many times do you change your opinion about something in your life, such as a food or a piece of clothing? Probably several times in your life, yet, each time you were convinced that you liked or disliked it. At the time, you were in full congruence with that statement and told someone else authentically what you believed. However, later on in your life you probably changed your opinion about that statement.

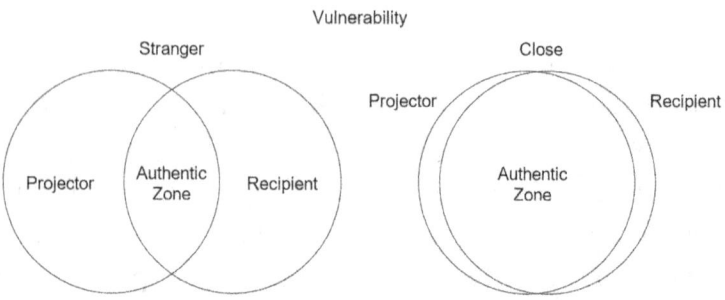

It does not mean that you were necessarily wrong initially, or what you are saying is not true. Hence, when you are developing the art of authenticity, you need to make sure that whatever you are saying, you ultimately believe that it is true regardless of its factual accuracy. Many people would probably disagree with that statement and argue that it is a matter of speaking truth. However, defining truth is a very complex topic that is more for a philosophical book than a business book.

## Vulnerability

Now if you were to follow the first two steps and go around the workplace being emotionally congruent with yourself and attuned to other people's reality, chances are you will be a very respected person. However, someone who speaks what they think is true and knows themselves is not always perceived as authentic. At times, they could be even considered emotionally distant. Imagine a manager in a company who followed the previous two steps to a T and was having a one-on-one conversation with an employee they managed. During the conversation, the manager would cover the employee's performance over the past month all based on facts such as:

"You were on time every day."

"You surpassed the deadline for the projects this quarter."

"You completed all the necessary training for your CEA certificate."

"You might be eligible for a promotion next quarter."

And so on. Now imagine a different type of conversation:

'It was great to see you were on time every day this quarter with the new baby in the house. I know that can be challenging so I just wanted to let you know I appreciate your consistency."

"Amazing that you surpassed the deadlines for this quarter, even though you had been pulled in so many other directions."

"Again, great job on getting that certificate training taken care of; you might be eligible for a promotion next quarter."

What was different? Do you feel that one manager was more authentic with their employee? Technically, both are equally authentic because they both stated the same amount of facts accurately. However, the big difference is derived from the emotion each manager displayed in their employee feedback. That extra ingredient to the authentic recipe is emotion, and emotion in a vulnerable sense. Here is where the feel-good language that will get a lot of the hard-edged managers rolling their eyes, because they believe they will lose respect by expressing their emotions. However, research mentioned earlier in this book stated that authentic leaders express a sense of vulnerability and, in order to reach this point of connection, emotion is needed when addressing others to be seen as someone authentic.

## Putting it All Together

Now we have learned all of the dimensions of authenticity and explained their relevance we can now visualize the end result as the diagram below. Each part playing an effective role in coming across as an authentic individual. Contrary to the original definition that authenticity is just the top circle - congruence, there is also attunement and vulnerability when addressing people. Missing one of the circles will inhibit one's ability to come across as authentic.

Each circle plays an important role later on this book when we look at the different parts of parts of the workplace. For now, we have a better and more refined version of what authenticity means to venture through the world to hand real life situations in the workplace. However, with this new knowledge, a lot of people will be wondering, well that's great, but how do I tangible act in that way in the workplace. Glad you asked, in the next chapter, we will dive into how to become authentic pulling apart each part of this definition and showing you the how-tos of making this a reality for you.

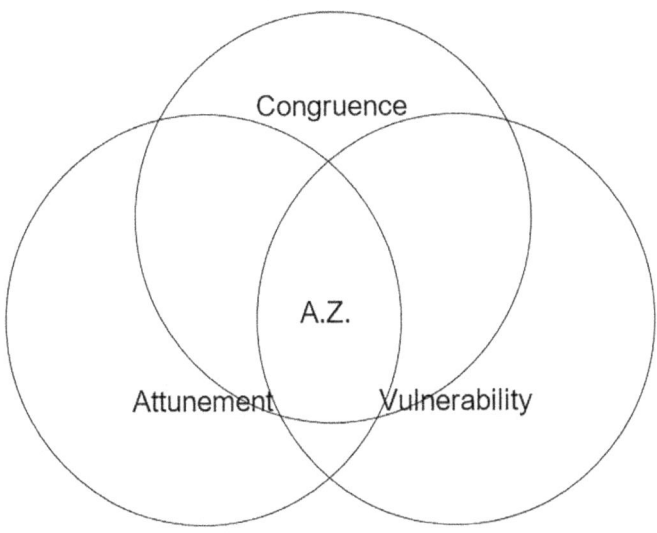

CHAPTER 3

# Becoming Authentic

*"Just say whatever comes to your mind."*

*"Speak up, there's no such thing as a dumb question."*

*"Just be yourself, everyone else is taken."*

**WHENEVER I READ** quotes like these, I always think of what would Phineas Gage (1823-1860) say if he were to follow one of these pieces of advice. Gage was the first of five siblings born in a small town in Grafton County, New Hampshire. During his youth, he was introduced to explosives on farms or nearby mines and soon fell in love with the dangerous profession. He eventually decided to make a living with explosives and he began working for a construction company near the Hudson River Railroad near Cortlandt Town, New York.

On September 13, 1848, Gage and a crew of men were working on a new project in Cavendish, Vermont, and he had the task of breaking apart a boulder blocking the work development. Gage set a blast site on a rock that was visible at the surface level, where he added the blast powder and fuse to the appointed position. He set everything and eventually the site was ready to be lit.

When he was about to light the fuse, someone asked him a question about the project. Out of respect, Gage stood up and at that very instant a rock scraped the tamping iron, lighting the powder, and consequently setting off a chain reaction to a massive explosive. A rod approximately an inch in diameter, three feet long and roughly 13 pounds shot straight into Gage's skull on the right up the left part of his jaw and through the top of his head. The iron landed some 80 feet away covered in Gage's warm blood and brain.

Gage collapsed to the ground, convulsed for a brief moment and then attempted to speak a few words shortly after. A few of his coworkers who watched the whole scene, reacted by picking Gage up, putting him on a stretcher and taking him off the work site to a safe location. While Gage was being taken away, he sat upright with some understanding of his surroundings. A doctor eventually came, fixed Gage up, and took him to a nearby hospital for his long recovery.

Surprisingly, after ten weeks of recovery, Gage was able to return home, and once a few weeks past, he was able to help out on the farm by doing simple tasks. However, Gage's friends and family noticed he was behaving differently, so a few psychologists took a closer look at him and recorded the difference. In the *Publications of Massachusetts Medical Society, they* stated:

"The equilibrium or balance, so to speak, between his intellectual faculties and animal propensities, seems to have been destroyed. He is fitful, irreverent, indulging at times in the grossest profanity (which was not previously his custom), manifesting but little deference for his fellows, impatient of restraint or advice when it conflicts with his desires, at times pertinaciously obstinate, yet capricious and vacillating, devising many plans of future operations, which are no sooner arranged than they are abandoned in turn for others appearing more feasible. A child in his intellectual capacity and manifestations, he has the animal passions of a strong man. Previous to his injury, although untrained in the schools, he possessed a well-balanced mind, and was looked upon by those who knew him as a shrewd, smart business man, very energetic and persistent in executing all his plans of operation. In this regard his mind was radically changed, so decidedly that his friends and acquaintances said he was "no longer Gage"

Essentially, the rod removed part of the brain that influenced Gage's personality that made him act like a completely different person. In Freudian psychology, Gage was now acting like the 'id,' the impulsive side of the personality that does not have any filter. It is the part that you resort to when you are angry, aroused or simply scared. As we mature, we learn how to better live with the 'id' part of our personality becoming more censored and deliberate in our actions.

The Gage story is famous in the field of psychology because, not only did he survive the incident, but he had a particular part of his brain removed that dramatically changed his personality. When relating this story to authenticity, Gage was a perfect example of someone who lacked the ability to acknowledge social cues and simply did whatever he felt like, what was true to him, or better yet, what was authentically him. Gage is a perfect example of an authentic individual according to the first conceptions of "just being yourself." Considering the quotes in the beginning, I could only imagine what Gage would say if someone said "Just say whatever comes to your mind." His response would be quite entertaining but probably wouldn't make much sense, however it would be *authentically* him.

How do you leverage modern authenticity and avoid coming off like a "Gage"? In this chapter, each sphere of authenticity [attunement, congruence, vulnerability] will be expanded into the why and how, providing practical tips in order to learn authenticity as an individual within the workplace of tomorrow.

## Building Emotional Congruence

One of the best ways to become more emotionally congruent is by increasing your understanding of who you are as a person. Unfortunately, there are various societal forces that will distort and color your perception of who you are. The challenge here is to overcome the environmental programming and learn how to tune into your internal voice which takes a considerable amount of effort. First off, let's list some of the strongest influencing forces in society and their impact on your identity.

## Familial Influence

Besides genetics, the most influential factor in shaping who one becomes is the family environment. While the home environment dramatically impacts the development of human beings, there are also ancestral pathology, or rather traits that are passed from generation to generation. There are two major factors to be concerned about when considering the influence family has on the individual. The first one is situational, the case-by-case parenting that takes place throughout adolescent development. These are things that parent's explicitly say in order to correct action, or in the parenting world, to discipline. The second is the modeling of behaviors that have been passed down from previous generations. As it is said, modeling is the best form of parenting and make it extremely difficult for children to break ancestral behavior patterns. A simple example can be seen with a child trying to be different from their alcoholic parents. *Psychology Today* mentioned this phenomenon by recording how it was more difficult for children to avoid being alcoholics if their parents were alcoholics.

The part where discovering yourself is tricky in the family environment is being able to discover your own voice. While I do not advocate abandoning the family structure, it is more important to learn about the influence of the family and understand that, very often when we tell ourselves to do certain things, it may come from respect for the family "extrinsic motivation" rather than our own "intrinsic motivation."

## Social Circle Influence

During early adolescence, peers are considered to be the most impressionable group according to a study published in *Global* titled *How Can Peer Group Influence the Behavior of Adolescents: Explanatory Model*. The study shows that most actions during that age are geared toward fitting in, making inauthenticity extremely prevalent. While another source, the Statistics *Portal*, found that 68% of teens experience peer pressure through social media. Consequently, the continuing use of these platforms in our society is suffocating the voices of the youngest in the journey to become more authentic.

Early adolescent development is also a period when children learn to become more social and, as a consequence, peer opinions have a bigger weight on their early decision-making. As adolescents mature, the influence of social circles tends to change in form from the peer's time in academia to when the younger parties are transitioning into adult life, according to Erik Erikson in *Identity and the Life Cycle*. In brief, early in life, the importance lies in the search for how to fit in with a social group. Later on, there is a perpetual urge to "keep up with the Jones." Regardless of what part of life, people inevitably act based on what they think their social group wants. Sometimes this leads them into a shallow life where they lack fulfillment because their values are externally driven by their peer groups rather than internally decided upon.

## Religious Influence

While religion may not have as much of an impactful role in society today compared with thousands of years ago, it still has a very strong influence on an individual's values. When considering religion with the lens of authenticity, one can take two paths: the first is to see a division between your values and a religion's values, while the second can be your values are your religion, hence you act in the way of your religion is authentic. The importance lies in feeling that we are in harmony with the path that we choose in life.

As society has become less reliant on religion, many philosophers have reflected on the possible effects this shift has had on society. One of the most important world-renowned thinkers about this impact is Friedrich Nietzsche, who became famous for his controversial opinions such as:

> "God is dead. God remains dead. And we have killed him. How shall we comfort ourselves, the murderers of all murderers? What was holiest and mightiest of all that the world has yet owned has bled to death under our knives: who will wipe this blood off us? What water is there for us to clean ourselves? What festivals of atonement, what sacred games shall we have to invent? Is not the greatness of this deed too great for us? Must we ourselves not become gods simply to appear worthy of it?"

The quote above has been often cited by the most radical thinkers, who have seen in the sentence "God is dead" the triumph of atheism. The rest of the quote seems to hide a more obscure meaning, religion is not dead because for centuries it had been the foundational pillar to our beliefs. If removed, it can cause the heart of our existence to come into question. Consequently, religion is not only the compass that we follow to understand morality and ethics, but the method that we use to fill in the blanks of the unexplainable lines about the world that we live in — a way to forgive the unforgivable. Religion is alive because it still has such a deep root in our ability to understand the world that, even today, it is imperative to still mention its influence. In essence, how much you choose to use it will determine the amount of influence it has on your life, for some it might not have a particular meaning but for others it will mean their entire inner world.

*Please note that I am not advocating the reader to abandon religion to understand who one is; rather I am only stating its importance on the shaping it has on an individual's values.*

## Political Influence

Political campaigns are run to attract attention by politically polarizing issues usually aimed at dividing audiences based off of temperament. Political leaders also want to align groups that turn into movements against a specific cause in order to create voters. While this strategy is solely to build attention and build a following, it has a dramatic impact on the individual who is observing the campaign. With the rise of social media, politics can impact someone's life from a psychological perspective more than ever before. In *Psychology Today,* Douglas LaBier Ph.D states:

"Now, some new research sheds light on a previously unrecognized link between fear, its source, and just how it shapes one's political position on polarizing issues. But I think these findings point to something beyond politics: That fear plays a much broader but overlooked role that in many facets of people's lives – including career dilemmas, conflicts around personal values, and problems in intimate relationships. Many fears are subtly conditioned by society's norms and family pressures. They remain largely unconscious, and can fuel a range of emotional conflicts and dilemmas about life-shaping decisions."

In other words, be wary because politics can be deep water to tread when it comes to psychological well-being and can also have a massive effect on the ones who don't care about politics.

## Media Influence

In order for media to survive, it must attract eyeballs which means creating the most attention-grabbing information possible, whether or not it is positive. In addition, the longer your attention is held, the more money they are able to make from advertisements. Hence, the system is set up for media to be alarming, catchy and requiring the viewers to be hyper-vigilant and concerned about the world. Steven Pinker, again in the *The Blank Slate,* described the reason why the media is extremely negative. This is due to a weakness of people and their ability to judge the probability of negative events, as he states:

"The nature of news is likely to distort people's view of the world because of a mental bug that the psychologists Amos Tversky and Daniel Kahneman called the Availability heuristic: people estimate the probability of an event or the frequency of a kind of thing by the ease with which instances come to mind. In many walks of life this is a serviceable rule of thumb."

Point being is that people tend to have a loophole in their mind that is acutely sensitive to negative news for precautionary safety reasons. Hence, if you want to be emotionally congruent, please stop watching so much news, because it is set up to fill your mind with negativity distorting your sense of reality and what is important.

## How Programming Develops - The Start of Inauthenticity

As discussed in the previous section, there are various avenues that inauthenticity stems from. This is in part driven by Watson/BF Skinner psychoanalytic theories assuming that "you can make a man out of any child if you change the upbringing." However, as more psychology research was published, we inevitably found out that people are not *infinitely* malleable but still possess the ability to make some degree of change.

With that said, when considering programming and the magnitude of emotional impact it has, one should consider feedback in three tiers.

- **Frequency:** The amount of times that you are told something.

- **Magnitude:** The impact of the statement. Commenting on someone's shoelace color is a lot less impactful than criticizing someone's existence

- **Source:** The person delivering the feedback. How close they are to you will determine the intensity of the feedback. Consider your mother/father versus an anonymous internet comment.

Over time, feedback begins to engrain itself in the mind, as it works to find safe ways to navigate the world by minimizing pain/maximizing pleasure while in pursuit of a goal.

Eventually, the world in which you live and believe to be true becomes assembled structures in the mind through neuro association. To imagine what this looks like, each belief, or rather assumption, about the world can be thought of as the top of a table. If the feedback resonates with the belief [table head], an extra leg is added to the table, that leg being the instance of the resonating memory and consequently strengthening the table. In cases where something is contrary to a belief, the legs of the table are lashed out weakening the strength of the table or belief. If the source is impactful enough, the belief structure collapses and the mind will then need to assemble a new structure in move forward.

This can also be thought of a different way employing the existentialism psychology. Its main premise defines purpose in order to shoulder the inevitable suffering that life brings. In other words, having a belief system that is strong enough to bear a suffering reality. With that strength, it can be said that the beliefs are the wood pieces that are holding up the house of your mind, strengthening it with every new piece. The nails that bind the pieces of wood are the associative experiences you had, and the strength of the nail is the magnitude of the event that is related to that belief. The strength of the associations are between individual pieces of parts of your mind. Eventually, a house that is built is a part of the feedback that you received from the world regarding the social dos and don'ts. This limits your ability to act in different ways, fearing that you will repeat a mistake you have made in the past; even though it could very well limiting your ability to be authentic. Who you are is not the house that was built, but the authentic you is what is within the house.

In the world of psychology, there are different schools of thought that explain why people need belief systems. Terror Management Theory, as set out in *Psychology Today,* frames this as "A type of defensive human thinking and behavior that stems from our awareness and fear of death. According to TMT, death anxiety drives us to adopt worldviews that protect our sense of self-esteem, worthiness and sustainability and allow us to believe that we play an important role in a meaningful world." While cynical at its core, a more positive approach mentioned earlier is existentialism where people are able to proactively define their meaning in life by creating a belief system strong enough to withstand the darkest of times.

Now we have a thorough grasp of how our mental programming develops in addition to having an awareness of how environment influences the ability to be authentic. The mind builds walls of limits in order to keep us safe both physically and emotionally by creating walls through past experiences.

## Congruence - Acting As Who One is

If you believe that I can go on to show you how to discover your true self, you will be sadly mistaken. In fact, I would be skeptical of anyone who says that they can do this for you. "Discovering oneself" might be one of the most difficult processes to go through, so don't expect any magic bullets in this section. There will definitely be several good nuggets and ways to help you make progress on your journey, but the unfortunate reality is, many people are on different parts of their journey of discovering who they are. It is best to assume that discovering who you truly are is indeed possible but know that each person's path is divinely unique.

In order to be authentic, we need to recall the base argument about Emotional Congruence- *It does not matter if you know who you truly are, it only matters if you truly believe the action or thought you have is truly yours in your heart of hearts.*

As cynical as that may sound, there is strong reasoning for that statement. First off, earlier in the book I explained the struggle of knowing who you truly are into a few main points.

- **Freudian Psychology:** You may do, think and feel things that you are not consciously aware of making your present self a reflection of your past experiences rather than your divine self.
- **Social Influence:** Where does the line stop between your unique ideas and someone else's?
- **Noble Savage:** What you consider for good might not be so at your deepest core?

In the world of authenticity, there are two major reasons to be authentic. The first is for the internal integrity of knowing you are doing the right thing, and the other is being perceived as authentic in order to gain the social benefits such as trust. With these two reasons, knowing who you truly are can often be referred to as a moving target. That might be your opinion today, but it could change the next day. Hence, focusing on how you can be emotionally congruent will be a better use of your time if you want others to perceive you as authentic. This is primarily due to the 55/38/7 principle discussed earlier. If you are emotionally congruent with what you are saying, people will assume you are being authentic.

Below are a few ways to know if you are being emotionally congruent:

- **Know yourself:** Someone who lives with congruency acts in direct accordance with their dreams, desires, beliefs, values, mission and goals. Hence, knowing the goals that you desire is paramount to becoming congruent.

- **Keep a journal:** From here, you can record your reflections internally or on the world. Just the act of writing down the ideas will give you a better understanding of how you feel and will be able to aid your ability to psychologically process events.

- **Kinesthetic Awareness:** What does your body feel? Make sure that if something feels a bit off in your body, that is a good indicator that you should ask yourself why.

- **The 5 Whys:** Asking yourself 5 'whys' repeatedly of 'why' you do what you're doing and 'why' you feel that way can uncover your true intentions quickly.

To put all of these together in order to tell if you are being authentic, first pause and feel how the action you just performed resonates with your body. Once you have performed the action, you can journal and ask yourself the 5 whys to get to know yourself and understand if you are being emotionally congruent. Journaling can also work as a great way of also unearthing your deep-rooted values.

While the past few points will help you become more emotionally congruent, here a few notes worth mentioning about discovering who you are:

- Becoming yourself is an iteration process.
- Discovering yourself requires both being in unusually difficult circumstances and reflecting on those events.
- Discovering who you are is similar to discovering your untapped potential.

It can be said that finding out who you are is like traveling through the world of difficult circumstances and finding out what you are truly capable of and what you are able to accomplish. This journey follows the traditional heroic archetype where the epic hero must go through an odyssey in order to find himself and to be reborn as their true self; in other words, finding out who they truly are is the whole purpose of their journey. Continuing to move through the adversities throughout life will enable you to eventually see your true authentic self as it surfaces.

## Attunement - Utilizing Empathy

As discussed earlier, empathy is immensely important in this journey because the act of being authentic involves the right connection to the other person's reality. Simply saying whatever comes to mind is not enough. For instance, going up to people who are overweight and telling them that they should watch their weight may be an authentic action because that is exactly what you are thinking. But it will not be truly authentic by today's perspective. Instead would just come off as obnoxious and emotionally void.

For individuals who may struggle with empathy, here are some questions and exercises that people can do to build that empathy muscle. When I was growing up, my parents used to ask me questions to help me develop empathy that were very irritating at the moment. But now that I look back, I understand the benefits. They were helping me develop a foundation of understanding of other people's reality, the first building block of empathy.

When you approach a situation where someone else has a different perspective, try these tips:

## 1. Listen

Why would I include something that most people would think is obvious? Because without this step, no empathy can take place. I am not referring to listening just with your ears, but rather, listening for any sort of signals or insights. Gestures such as a repulsed-looking face when talking about a subject, probably means they don't agree, even though they may verbally say they do. Watching someone's actions can be one of the best ways of determining someone's inner thoughts. As Ralph Waldo Emerson famously said, "your actions speak so loudly, I cannot hear what you are saying."

After you have listened you will be able to take the next step.

## 2. Put aside your viewpoint and try to see things from the other person's point of view.

The most widely known approach to empathy is putting yourself in someone else's shoes. While this is common knowledge, nowadays we continuously find ourselves struggling to understand each other. Being able to understand another person's view involves completely entering the other person's world while forgetting your own for an instant. Once you are able to put yourself into the other person's shoes, you will need to ask yourself continuously: in what circumstances does their behavior make sense? You can swap out different causation patterns and eventually you will be able to crack the code of their worldview. It may not be in line with your beliefs and values, but you will understand the world by a different set of rules.

After a good amount of practice, the ability to understand another person's reality will become much easier. Stick with it and you will be surprised by your understanding of different people's reality. Fictional writers often use this technique to figure out how their characters should act in the world in realistic and believable ways. In order to build a character, writers need to address a few major pillars which are also essential to putting yourself in someone else's shoes. Some of these techniques are sitting down with imaginary characters and asking them questions about themselves to discover what they should do in the story. The questions that the writers use are similar to what you should be asking yourself. A few of them goes as follows:

1. *What are this person's needs, desires, ambitions and goals? Do these change throughout time?*

    People are goal-seeking creatures and understanding what their ambitions are is key to understanding the main driving force of their reality. If they react in a certain way in a situation, by finding what motivates them, it will become much easier to understand why they react as they do.

2. *Do I have any bias toward this individual? Or better yet, does this person remind me of anyone or anything that I despise?*

    So here is where most people get tripped up. Throughout the empathetic process, many people would get to step 3 and start to judge the other person's intentions or actions. Often, our beliefs are embedded in past events that make sense to us but not to the other party. Hence, understanding our bias toward another person is immensely helpful in outlining their true intentions.

3. *Do I lose anything if this person is right?*

    Again, this question is aimed at bias. Sometimes you don't want the other person to be right in their perspective because it may mean you are wrong. So discovering what skin you have in the game is super-important to learning what your stance is in the situation. What often happens in deploying empathy is that you begin to understand where others come from and, on occasion, realize that you might have been wrong in a certain situation. However, in order to avoid loss, you will keep your same position and unfortunately, avoid being empathetic.

4. *Lastly, if you don't know what they are feeling in a certain situation, ask.*

    The next time you are in a situation where you are curious about the other person's reality, make sure to run through this list of steps. After a bit of practice, the steps will be ingrained into your subconscious and you will have a great understanding of what drives the other person and how to be authentically you in their presence.

Hopefully, through those 4 steps, you will have a much easier time in deploying attunement to the person you are addressing. While they seem easier on the surface, having empathy for another individual and truly understanding where they are coming from is truly an art that takes years of practice. However, over time, your skills will rise to where empathy will become automatic and you will understand what to say in order to come across as authentic to the person.

## Vulnerability- Expressing Emotion

Erin Weed, in her Google Talk, referenced Authenticity as having three parts: head, heart and desire. Head being the logic of what has happen, heart is the emotion behind what you do, and desire is why you want to do something. However, I would argue that authenticity is about having emotion when addressing a problem. This can simply come from attaching emotion to what you are saying by using 'I feel' similar to what Eric Weed has in her heart part of her authenticity triangle. Another way you can deploy emotion is in feedback in your response to a situation using the 4 Step Nonviolent Communication developed by Marshall Rosenberg PhD, a communications coach and mediator for civil rights and student activists during the US civil rights era.

Rosenberg developed a practical strategy for peaceful conflict resolution called non-violent communication (NVC). By focusing on language and process, the theory goes, injured parties can shift the tone of their communication and spur collaboration instead. However, in cases of this book, we will be focusing more on the way that this kind of language can have an emotional impact on someone. These four steps are:

1. **Observe and recap**

   The NVC process begins with neutral observation. In conversations, this is most easily done by recapping what someone has said, without emotional input. That means not attaching any judgment to your response such as comments that begin in the first person, i.e. "I hear you say" work better than "You just said."

   Example:

   Person 1: *"We have to do something about the illegal immigrant problem, because they're taking away our jobs, and people act like you don't care."*

   Person 2: *"I'm hearing what you say that you're worried about your job security and that other people in this country are ignoring that concern."*

   This tool slows the pace of conversation, and forces both sides to reflect and clarify.

2. **Describe emotions, not positions**

   Talk feelings, not issues. If you're trying to make yourself heard, clearly describe your own emotions, rather than your positions. In the immigration example above, for instance, the second person might ask: "Are you feeling frightened and disrespected?" rather than stating that immigrants are entitled to certain rights. The hard part in nailing this step is expressing only your own emotional turmoil, rather than translating your emotions into blame. By contrast, "I feel like" is typically used to express opinions, not feelings. Even "I feel misunderstood," expresses "You misunderstood me," and lays subtle blame. "I feel hurt" is also a trap; it implies that the other person has done something wrong.

3. **Identify needs**

   According to NVC teachings, all of the emotions we experience when we're upset are connected to an unmet need, which is a requirement for contentment. Rosenberg found that human needs universally fall into one of a handful of categories, including connection, honesty, peace, play, physical well-being, a sense of meaning, and autonomy. A person concerned with an immigration crackdown might say,

   *"I want to be confident that my family and I have some stability."*

   *The other party might ask, "Are you looking for awareness for the situation you're in?"*

4. **Make a request**

   At a certain point in the conversation, it's time to ask for concrete actions that would help satisfy a need. At this point, you are putting together all of the information you have gathered in the previous steps and are putting forward a proposition that encompasses the other people's reality.

*"Would you like to...?"*

*"Would you be willing to...?"*

If you are not in a situation of giving feedback, sometimes just using this model for addressing your concerns about a situation is immensely important. Note that there are boundaries to using "I feel" statements. Sometimes people take this "I feel" stuff way too far and begin having a mushy vibe that causes most people to feel uncomfortable in their presence.

From this section, you learned two methods for deploying emotion when addressing others, the first is simply using some heart in how you are describing some need, and the second is Non-Violent Communication. Both are very useful in bringing in more emotion. If you are curious about the Non-Violent Communication in more detail, I highly recommend reading Rosenberg's book, *Nonviolent Communication.*

## Staying on the Path of Authenticity

Now that you have a solid grasp of authenticity and its three dimensions, you will find occasionally that when you act authentic, people won't always respect your intentions. In fact, they may even be repulsed by your actions, responding with negative criticism in some form that will most likely drive you back into your metaphysical shell of inauthenticity. Or rather, being reluctant to share what you believe. Negative feedback is inevitable no matter how excellent you are at communicating with authenticity, therefore, here are a few ways to handle negative feedback and keep you on the path of striving for authenticity.

- The first way you can accomplish this is by understanding the other person's frame of mind. In the previous section, we discussed how to empathetically understand someone else's reality. That same technique can help you discover why certain people respond the way they do. In such cases, you will often find that the other people may be responding in ways that have little or nothing to do with you.

- The second way you can accomplish this is through separating action from self. If you were to take care of a friend's child who was learning how to ride a bike and for the life of them, they could not figure out how to ride it, what would you think of the child? Would you think that the child's ability to ride the bike was lacking or the child was in their entirety bad? Very often we are encountered with the same question when we may make a mistake in a social situation where we say the wrong thing at the wrong time and we erroneously conclude that we are bad as a whole because of something we did, rather than concluding that the action wasn't appropriate. In cognitive behavior therapy, this is often referred to as "overgeneralization" where you do one thing wrong and that one action somehow becomes your entire identity. Essentially, you overgeneralize the significance of that action in your life.

CHAPTER 4

# Attracting Top Talent with Authenticity

By most people's standards, she was considered very attractive.

At the time, Kate was looking for a new job in user interface design and was interviewing with various startups in San Francisco. She already had a job, but felt underpaid in spite of having a strong resume in hand that listed her experience with reputable companies. For that reason, Kate started searching for a better job, with a more desirable salary and benefits. Over a month, she had been to more than a dozen interviews and now she had reached the final round interview for a startup located in south SOMA county in San Francisco.

Her interview at the startup began at 10 a.m. so she made sure to show up at 9:45 at the front door, prepped with coffee in one hand and psychologically ready to handle a battery of questions. However, when she approached the company's tall blue door, no one was there to greet her. She knocked on the door but, because of its density, no one heard her knock. She checked her phone to see if she could call the recruiter to let her in, but the recruiter didn't work for the company she was interviewing with, so a call would not be very helpful.

After waiting alone and outside the building for 10 minutes, someone from the company walked outside for a smoke break. As the door began to close, Kate grabbed the door and walked inside. But soon, she felt confusion since, as she looked around, she could not tell who was part of the team that she was interviewing with because she never met anyone in person. Frazzled not only by the isolation but also the loud noise that came from everyone talking loudly, Kate inevitably realized that she was in a cubicle field of cold callers. Not wanting to disturb them, she sat down at the kitchen area, next to the cubicle field and put her purse down on the table. She realized that the table was not clean when she noticed that her purse was placed in a small pool of ketchup. Immediately she rushed over to clean up the unexpected mess. Then someone interrupted her by asking: "Are you Kate?"

Surprised, she responded yes, and the employee introduced himself as the first interviewer, and he walked his way upstairs with an embarrassed Kate behind, since she did not have enough time to clean her purse. But that was just the beginning of her problems. She soon realized that the company was not very organized, and they wanted the whole engineering team to interview Kate individually, with no rhyme or reason for the interview questions, which lead to an exhausting 8-hour interview. After this, she was overwhelmed and tired and finally the last person told her that she could go. Without delay, Kate grabbed her ketchup stained purse and walked out the door that she initially entered and into the night.

Originally, Kate did not recognize the surroundings because it was a dark night. However, she abruptly concluded that it was an alleyway filled with danger. Having entered there in the day time and more worried about the interview, she did not notice where the company was located. But the night revealed a sleeping ground for the homeless and drug addicts. The ground was cluttered with needles, trash, human waste and broken glass. Completely wiped out from a long day of interviews, and now fearing for her safety, she began to run down the alley to a more lit street, until she found herself out of danger and remembered breathing.

With the light of a new day, she got a call from the company and was told that they wanted to extend a job offer. While excited, she felt a very negative vibe about the company and told them that she would let them know in the next couple of days if she would accept. For many days, Kate thought about the positive and negative aspect of the new job offer. On one hand, the new offer was much higher than what she currently had and in spite of the long hours of interview, she really liked the people there. However, on the other hand, something was off. Eventually, she realized that being left outside both before and after the interview really distorted her thinking. But since they offered her a pretty paycheck, she decided to finally accept.

This was a true story of a co-worker at a company I used to work for and the experience of interviewing at the company we both worked at. Both of us almost did not accept because there were things about the company that really did not sit well with us, such as the location and the care that was taken in the interview process. The eight hours were unnecessary, and we were both left in a relatively dangerous alleyway. It was overall a negative experience, but the pay was good and the people were nice so we both accepted.

## The Shift to Authenticity

The old traditional job ad in the United States consisted of putting an ad in the newspaper. First, candidates would then apply for that job, then interview in person or over the phone, and finally they would receive a job offer. This used to be a fairly straightforward process, but, due to the immense amount of advancements in the world of technology, the recruitment process has opened up to changes that companies can use in their advantage. Authenticity, in the dimension of attunement, will help dramatically with a lot of these changes as we will see later in this chapter.

Before we disclose what part of the recruitment process is being impacted, it would be helpful to disassemble the recruitment process into tangible pieces, then analyze each one with a lens of authenticity. The tangibles pieces that we will use to structure the recruitment process are: attention, interest, and commitment.

The attention phase consists of the candidate becoming aware of the company itself and making the commitment to start the job interview process. The second part, interest, is where the candidates begin to go through the job interview process. Finally, commitment is where the candidate is offered a job and they have the choice of accepting, negotiating or declining. In the beginning of the recruitment process, most candidates are in the attention phase or rather on the top of the funnel. Over time, the candidates are weeded out through the different interviews to where only a select few or single one is offered a job (commitment).

From a numeric point of view, here is what you would typically look at: 300-500 people apply for a tech job [Attention], 50 get the first-round behavioral interview [Interest], 30 make it to the technical interview [interest], 10 onsite [interest], 3 job offers [Commitment], 1 acceptance [Commitment].

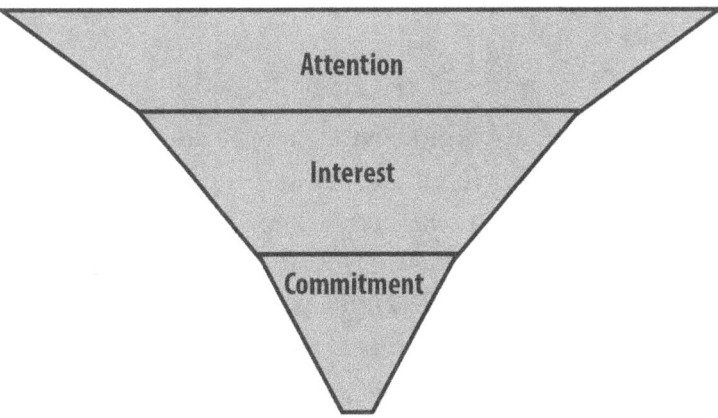

In 2018, we are currently in a bull economy, meaning there are more jobs than there are people to fill them, employers need to make sure that the interview and recruitment processes are right so that when those ideals candidates walk through the door, the company is putting their best foot forward.

How do they make sure they are putting their best foot forward? I recommend that they do this by going through the job interview process themselves and seeing if they are making it an enjoyable experience. I am not saying there should be limo service and catered 5-star restaurant food, but rather putting a small amount of effort forward can go a long way in the candidate's ultimate decision.

Throughout this chapter, we will be exploring the job recruitment process and how authenticity applies to each part of the funnel in addition to how authenticity is becoming a more critical part in the recruitment process in the future. Note, these techniques will help you regardless of the size of the company or organization you work for.

## Phase 1: Attention

Obtaining a candidate's attention can be done in two ways: through the known job market and the hidden job market. Most people are aware of the known job market, which is when a job ad goes up on a website such as Glassdoor, Indeed or LinkedIn or any other of the dozens of jobs websites, and anyone can apply through these sites. Now, it does not have to be websites, anywhere public where a job is posted is considered the known job market.

On the other hand, the hidden job market is the part of the market where jobs *are not* posted and the opening is only known internally instead of externally. The hidden job market accounts for approximately 80% of the jobs out there according to *Forbes*. With such an astounding figure, the importance of having employees who will tell their friends about the company they are working for cannot be underestimated. How to do that effectively will be covered later in the book.

In 2018, a lot of organizations struggle to attract ideal candidates because of their inability to prioritize between new salary and benefit expectation. Due to the current bull market, it becomes easier for candidates to request obscene things of companies and expect them to jump through hoops to hire them. Each candidate has a series of questions that they ask themselves about the company they are searching for. Usually this starts with money, culture, team, and career opportunity. When every company is offering those same things, the little differences between the companies start to make the biggest difference.

That is one of the reasons why the bean bag culture started to become so popular. Companies were literally jumping over each other to impress future candidates by adding superficial items to the workplace, like catered food, game rooms, and bean bags. As soon as one company started offering a benefit, it becomes an expectation for other companies. It essentially becomes a cycle with companies constantly having to update their offers to cater to the job market.

## The Details Matter

So how does a candidate make a decision on what company to start interviewing with if all the companies they are prospecting all have the same pay, reviews, brand size? The answer is a personal question, pun intended. Each individual person has a weighted. multi-variable question in their mind to test the attributes of the companies and how much they prefer those attributes. To tap into the liking meter, companies need to learn how to harness their ability to be relatable and understand the candidate, implying that authenticity is imperative for this connection. When candidates have a surplus of options, sometimes due to the economy or other times because the candidate is proficient and in demand for what they do, they begin to look at other things besides pay and benefits.

In the bestselling book, *Talent Magnet - How to Attract and Keep the Best People,* Miller conducts a research project with the consulting company AON, a global leader in human resources, and Prophet, a global brand agency focusing on solving the question of what attracts top talent. The study had more than 7,000 participants across 50 states in the United States, included all age groups from as young as 14 to as old as 65. In addition, they looked at both blue- and white-collar job applicants and various educational backgrounds. Various methods were used to extract the data such as live interviews, ethnography, quantitative survey, and multi-stage panel surveys.

Warning and spoiler alert: what the author found through this elaborate study is that personal growth, mission and values, and a better boss were all things that top talent looked for, more so than typical talent did. However, while wage and payment were important to top talent, the top talent individuals did not weigh this as heavily when considering future employment. When I first came across this study, I could not make sense of why certain attributes attracted top talent did were not as important for typical applicants. Why would this particular group of attributes be weighted higher than things such as wage and benefits? There were people who joined companies for reasons other than the pay, but what did this say about the individual?

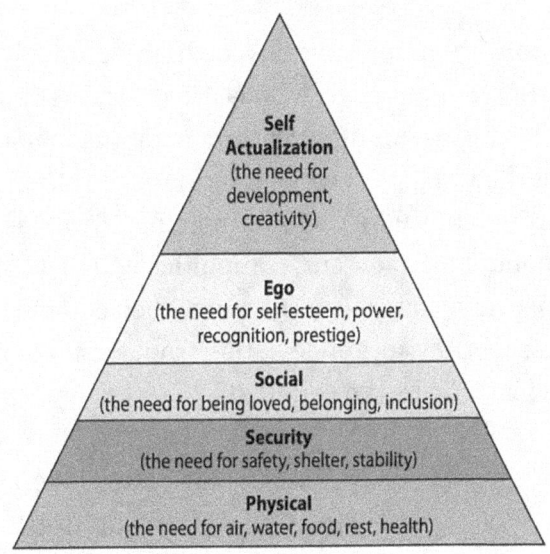

After pondering about this study for some time, I made sense of it through comparing it to Maslow's hierarchy. The hierarchy itself was originally coined by Abraham Maslow in order to derive meaning by what human's are motivated by. If one would look at the top of the pyramid, they would see a direct resemblance to the items that attract top talent versus typical talent. Going up the pyramid, typical talent attractors such as wage, immediate culture, and brand were at the very bottom, physical, security and social. While the top is consistent with what attracted the top talent: personal growth, self-actualization, ego, mission and values, self-actualization, external company leadership.

The conditions that attract top talent individuals were identical to the needs of high actualizing individuals in the Maslow's Hierarchy.

In addition, companies need to be high-actualizing to attract self-actualizing individuals. However, the concept of authenticity is becoming ever important in companies because of the importance of career path or rather, having an environment that is "self-actualizing." By invoking the component of attunement, companies will be able to create rapport and congruence because when communicating that message, any sort of deviation from the main mission will be picked up by the candidate.

A leader *not* usually known for authenticity, Elon Musk, does a great job of attracting the best talent in the world to work at Tesla. Tesla, notoriously known to pay their workers below average wages , has Musk lead them in a very authentic way: "No words can express how much I care about your safety and well-being," Musk wrote. "Going forward, I've asked that every injury be reported directly to me, without exception. I'm meeting with the safety team every week and would like to meet every injured person as soon as they are well, so that I can understand from them exactly what we need to do to make it better. I will then go down to the production line and perform the same task that they perform." Reading that same article, some would argue that he is doing a PR stunt. However, no one can argue that there has been an enormous about of hype and excitement about his projects, Tesla and SpaceX have attracted the top talent around the world regardless of the pay involvement. Further weighing on the importance of how applicants are able to attract top talent to their company by them focusing on the mission and values of the companies.

John Maxwell, an internationally known leadership author, supports the difficulty of getting people to follow in a mission when there is not strong pay, as he would often reflect upon for his consistent work in the church space, which was completely volunteer. More applicably to Elon Musk though, Maxwell says "People buy into the leader, before they buy into the vision." For Tesla to attract talent, they are able to leverage Musk as the hero of the company. People believe in him, so thousands of people apply to positions at his companies. This is simply the company leading with a strong value proposition that is focused on what will attract top talent.

## Creating a Strong Value Proposition

*Has this happened to you?* There is a shortage of talent so the executive team, along with the head recruiters, brainstorms ways to attract talent, including how they will change the value propositions (what they tell potential candidates) that they send out into the world. The recruiting team goes off into the field, blasting potential candidates with in-mails on LinkedIn, or handling various calls pitching the same value proposition that was covered in the meeting. However, at the end of the day, there is no change. Or better yet, *have you interviewed with a company and the story that the recruiter told you about the company didn't sound interesting at all and was the jumble of a bunch of corporate talk?* If this has happened to you, you are not alone.

To this day, I still receive emails and occasional in-mails on LinkedIn regarding my employment status for software engineering. I would often read through the inquiry looking for how they use their copy so I can look for changes. More often than not, the value propositions — why I should join their company — is filled with a lot of corporate speak that does not resonate with me effectively.

A good friend of mine once said that all of the best candidates in the world are already working for someone, that means that you better have a very strong value proposition or reason for why they should leave their path and join you and your company.

So how do you create an enticing value proposition that can attract the top talent to your organization sprinkled with authenticity? The first thing that people need to know is how to get into the mind of the ideal candidate. In order to achieve this, two different methods can be used: qualitative and quantitative. Some studies used in the book mentioned earlier, *Talent Magnet*, revealed how top performers in the company were called into a room with the recruiting team and asked a battery of questions about why they work there. Then, lower-performing employees were brought into the same room and their answers were recorded. After the data was collected, the value proposition for both groups was evaluated.

The point of this exercise is to figure out key differences between the high/low performing groups so the firm can capitalize on what attracts the top talent. Often, people want to shortcut this process and just guess why people join the company. I heavily caution against that because often the reason why the executive team thinks that someone should work for a company is not the reason someone actually does. A candidate who is older might say that the company is very stable, and the benefits are solid, while someone who is much more junior might state that the company is located close to downtown. If you were trying to attract someone junior and the company does not do internal interviews, you might resort to value propositions that do not resonate with either a top-performing candidate nor a candidate of the demographic they are targeting.

While qualitative analysis is used for in-person interviews, quantitative research is done through companywide surveys using the same series of questions. I would suggest you leverage both, but if you had to choose one, go with qualitative because it's faster to bring a bunch of people into a room and interview them, and from personal experience, people rarely put as much effort into a survey as someone who is interviewing them. Note too, that in order to get real responses from employees, especially for the qualitative research, being authentic, or rather perceptively trustworthy when asking for responses, is imperative. People who are responding to your inquiries are going out on a limb because of the danger of what might happen if their true reasons for the being at the company are revealed.

Now that you are able to effectively create a strong value proposition, there is one way that you can take this one step further by filming the employee and uploading it to the job description. This is because, as mentioned before, through text communication, you only take into account the 7%. If you use video, you are able to get 100% of the 55/38/7 of the body language likeness. In other lines of work, there is usually an apex where a big moment happens in a career which is why they got into it in the first place. By filming someone and interviewing right or shortly after they experience this apex, you would create an amazingly authentic video to put on your website and in your job description by using authenticity to attract similar candidates. By filming such a video, the future candidate can see a high-performing individual go through the most exciting part of their career triggering likability in the candidate's mind.

To this day, I rarely see recruiters using video to their advantage in outreach to potential candidates. I suspect this method of communication, especially for recruiting, will be playing an ever-increasing role in the recruitment process of tomorrow, which would put a stronger emphasis on an authentic approach.

## Broadcasting the Message

Getting your ideal candidate to know about your job opening is easier than ever and it will be even easier in the future. Today there are various ways to reach candidates: LinkedIn, Glassdoor, Indeed, Snapchat, email, and dozens of other methods. Often the method of posting a job on these platforms is called passive recruiting, while reaching out to candidates directly through email and such is called active. Additionally, when leveraging a method, there are some important things you will need to consider:

- Since it is easier to reach candidates, that means candidates are easily bombarded by your competitors trying to do the same thing you are doing.
- Technology is often leveraged to reach candidates on a massive scale, which means personalization is now commonplace.

If you want to attract candidates and your company does not have a strong brand, the way you can cut through the noise is by being an early adopter — trying new things that are on the fringe. Why? Because you stand out. Simply allowing applicants to copy and pasting three companies they have worked for is no longer an attention-getter, for there are tons of tools today that enable fill templates. Today, more than ever, video is starting to make its debut in the recruitment process.

However, there is one very vital and important point to capitalize on when considering video. The concept is very simple yet often misunderstood for reasons I will delve into a bit later. However, there is an inverse relationship between production quality and connection.

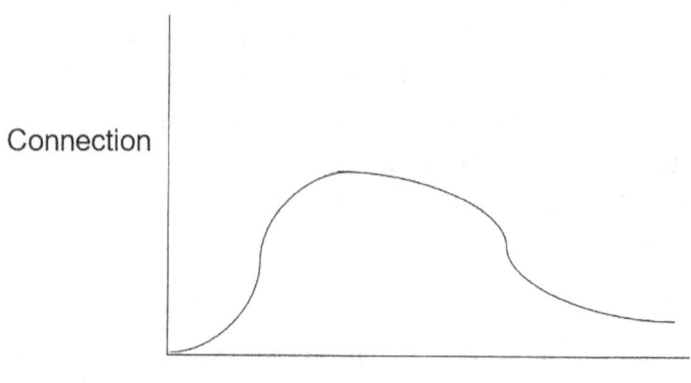

Why is this the case? Well, if you look at the vast majority of video content that is consumed today, it is done in semi-production state. Usually filmed on someone's phone, there is no b-roll, no mic hook up, just straight filming and go. Due to the quality increase in smartphone technology, anyone can create a good video with just their phone.

Companies commonly get tripped when they try to maintain a strong brand image by making a very professional and expensive recruiting video that includes: tons of b-roll, custom music and memorized scripts. In my keynotes, I often compare a high production recruiting video to a video filmed on someone's camera. Without failure, the smartphone-filmed video always wins. Almost every time, people prefer the lower quality video because it is much easier to relate to.

Tubular Insights has performed research in this field finding that more informal videos are shown to be easier to connect to. The tech company pointed out in The Martian, a science fiction movie that of course involves Mars and stars Matt Damon, had two different trailers, the first one was a very formal trailer with the deep voice-over and heavy cut scenes and the other was a simple video log of all of the astronauts on the space station. When comparing the two trailers, the vlog version gets about 40% more engagement, likes and comments per view than the traditional trailer. Demonstrating a colloration between engagement and more of an authentic feel to the video experience.

In addition, there are startling statistics from YouTube showing that 70% of teenagers say they resonate more with YouTube celebrities than traditional celebrities. Meaning that the informal person who is not world-famous who is filming videos in their room with no massive celebrity clothing line endorsement is resonating and building more trust than traditional celebrities. There are many cases for why this is the case, but the biggest one is that there are fewer barriers between the end user and the creator of content making for a stronger and more authentic connection.

So how does this relate to video quality and recruiting? Well, take note that the vast majority of content[11] consumed today is through social media, so people are used to consuming content that way. Which means that when you create a fancy high-production video, it can easily have the reverse effect of not connecting with your ideal candidate. Make sure you balance video production with the need to connect with your audience.

---

11   https://www.statista.com/statistics/565628/time-spent-digital-traditional-media-usa/

To conclude this section, here are a few tips to use when trying to find the ideal candidate

**Celebritization:** Many small companies are using social media to video log the CEO to create a stronger brand for recruitment (see Vaynermedia, 10x Rule, Bold Worldwide). All of these companies are able to bring authenticity and transparency to a new level by following an individual and showing everyday operations in their companies.

**Surge Referrals:** This is a technique that Lyft used to get more drivers and is also a handy trick for creating demand for a particular position. It involved having a large referral bonus for a select time frame period of only a few weeks.

**Pay for Referrals:** Putting on a job description ad that you will give a person a finder's fee for referring someone to your job who gets hired. Essentially, making internal referral fees, external.

**Video Job Description:** Including videos of actual employees giving testimonials of their experience working for the company you represent.

**Giphy Picture in Job Description:** An idea I found from another entrepreneur who used GIPHYs (small repeated images) in the outreach email campaign to give a more authentic touch to the receipt of the email. The company founder who initially suggested this idea found a 4x improvement in response rate after adding this extra touch. This leverages the attunement aspect of authenticity by making the outreach a more customized campaign.

# Building Interest in An Authentic Way

Once you have their attention, the task becomes how to filter through the candidates in the recruiting funnel. Depending on your industry and the level of position, job interviews can range from as short as one week with one onsite interview, to as long as six months for more senior positions consisting of dozens of interviews. Regardless of the number of rounds that someone goes through, it is important to ensure that, as they go through the interview process, you and the candidate acquire a more real, or rather, authentic feel for one another. By the end of the interview process, it needs to be clear whether or not it is a good fit. In this section, I will cover various strategies for not only building a candidate's interest in the job interview process, but also for helping you spot red flags early on in the recruitment process.

The first human interview in many companies is usually a behavioral interview. This is where the recruiter or hiring manager jumps on the phone with a candidate and figures out if the candidate can handle the job from a non-technical perspective. As someone who has been in more than 500 interviews, this is notoriously known to be the easiest part of the interview process. Why? Because they often ask questions that are very similar to other recruitments.

- Tell me about a time that you were in a difficult situation and how you resolved it?
- Why do you want to work here?
- What is your most proud achievement?

The problem with these questions is that, if you have a semi-smart candidate, chances are they will have already memorized the answers to these questions in order to tell you exactly what you want to hear. As most would say, a candidate with tell you everything you want to hear to get a job offer.

Many companies have struggled with this same problem with having candidates get through the interview process, but after they are working at the company, they seem to be completely different. So, what can companies do to improve this? Google has done probably more research in this field than any other company, simply because they have the sheer volume of candidates to do research on, analyzed the behavioral interview and found something obvious, yet hidden. During the typical behavioral interview, there are a series of questions that are normally asked, and should be asked. However, the trick is to apply situational questions to create an authentic response from the candidate.

What is a situational question?

- How would you handle a situation where a co-worker was upset and poured coffee all over your new shirt?

- Assume a co-worker really wanted to leave the company. Why do you think he would want to leave?

- You just helped the team accomplish over 50% of their quota in one week and you are announcing the news to your team. What do you say?

In order to vet questions, you need an authentic response, something that is truly them. That is why you need to create a pattern interrupt during the job interview process. Helen Roe describes it as "a technique to change a particular thought, behavior or situation. Behavioral psychology and neuro linguistic programming use this technique to interrupt and change thought patterns and behaviors. It can be as simple as initiating a handshake or as definitive as seizing the moment to travel or fulfill your bucket list." Having a candidate think on their feet is super-important to finding out their true wiring. The psychological reasoning for this is due to the fact that people will need to engage more of their subconscious mind during the assembling of their answer. It is not predetermined in the forefront of their mind, so as an interviewer, you will be able to get more of a natural response from the candidate.

Google also tried to increase the quality of the candidates they were accepting by having structured answers and criteria for all applicants. Throughout the Google process, the questions are determined ahead of time, and how the candidate does is determined by how many points they get by the end of the day. The main reasoning behind this is to avoid interviewer bias during the interview process. Often, candidates will resonate more with a particular employee, which tends to distort the psychological point tally the interviewer keeps in their head for the interviewee.

To further build on the structure interview, Google has a committee as a third party decide whether or not someone is acceptable for the Google family. The important part during this process is that the group has no contact with the candidate in order to avoid bias. They will look over everything from the point totals of the interviewers and the candidate's resume and vote to bring a candidate on board.

What someone might notice about this process is that Google, and many companies in general, are trying to remove the bias from the interview process. While many companies are doing a great job of this, people are inherently biased, which means a truly unbiased interview process can only come with no human involvement. But then, what is the likelihood that people will just accept someone new onto their team when they have absolutely no say in the decision, but Hal does? This by itself, will be one of the most difficult problems to solve in the up and coming future recruitment process. How do you create a truly unbiased interview with humans involved?

## Stacking Interviews

During the interest phase, each interview is supposed to be used as an obstacle that will remove the unqualified candidates and keep the best funneling through the system. However, candidates are often put through a sequencing of interviewing that is doing the reverse effect. For instance, there are three major types of technical interviews one can do:

- Technical Q&A phone screen
- Take-home project
- Online test

Each one of these avenues has its pros and cons.

| Interview Type | Pros | Cons |
|---|---|---|
| Technical Face-to-Face Q&A | ■ Can obtain contextual information about the candidate. | ■ Financially risky considering poor candidates.<br>■ Requires interviewer to ask relevant questions. |
| Take-home Project | ■ Can see how the candidate completes actual work.<br>■ Can measure commitment level to the company. | ■ If placed too early in the interview process, can weed out solid candidates if the company has a weak brand. |
| Online Test | ■ Cost-effective way of removing poor candidates. | ■ If the candidate is good with the internet, they will be able to overcome this round. |

Ultimately, the onsite interview is usually last; however I have interviewed with companies that have reversed the order, which seemed quite odd from a financial perspective. The goal of recruitment is to place these in the recruitment funnel to maximize interest but also filter out poor candidates. Usually the most common mistake I have seen in this project is in putting take-home projects too early in the interview process, or more specifically, when the company has a poor brand, they expect the candidate to complete a 5-10-hour project. The issue at hand is most candidates will stop interviewing with that company because they are not sold on moving forward with the company.

Now, this does have a beneficial effect, as Robert Cialdini in his book *Influence* points out in relation to hazing. He notes how this reflects the traditional "Hell Week" process held yearly in order to put the newest "pledges" or potential candidates through a series of difficult tasks before they are accepted into the house. Robert then mentions that Elliot Aronson and Judson Mills, two social psychologists, concluded that "persons who go through a great deal of trouble or pain to attain something tend to value it more highly than persons who attain the same thing with a minimum of effort." College groups that did require as difficult of an initiation process were considered "worthless and uninteresting." A bizarre effect, yet, understandable nevertheless.

This may seemed far-fetched to bring into a discussion about work environment interviews. During my college years, Palantir, a government data company, used to put engineers through the most intellectually challenging interviews possible. So much so that interviews at companies like Amazon and Google paled in comparison to the intensity of Palantir's. However, something interesting took place. When students tried to overcome these interviews, many would fail, making it a badge of honor, and also a credibility symbol if they were able to make it through the turmoil.

What I am implying here is that how you stack interviews in succession can create a series of effects for your candidate to get through, sometimes increasing the desire to work for you, other times, not as much.

As we move forward into the future, it will become easier and easier to apply to jobs. Some ads on LinkedIn literally suggest that you can answer a few questions and you will instantly receive job offers. I am not joking about this. However, as the difficulty of interviews decreases, the total number of people applying per company will increase, making it more important to stack interviews to make sure you get the right candidates.

## Creating an Unforgettable Experience Using Authenticity

By far, the onsite interview will play a role in the decision that your candidate makes about your company. Often, when companies have onsite interviews, they are not well thought out and they are held as a boiler room setting. A boiler room basically means that the candidate is put through a series of uncomfortable situations in order to find out what they are capable of. While this is a common technique in sales, it is not as common for engineering. One of the most important things to do with a candidate is to build a strong relationship with them. Why? Because Officevibe[12] found that 58% of men and 70% of women wouldn't take high pay for friends demonstrating that there is immense weight on how much relationships come into play with job decisions.

So how do you build a strong relationship with a candidate? Here are a few tips that I learned from interviewing companies:

---

12   https://blog.hubspot.com/marketing/workplace-friendships#sm.0001j685cegfndl3tsy2raauuy3ip

First, put the most charismatic person from the team that the candidate is interviewing with in front of the building to greet the candidate. Often, companies have the recruiter go out and greet the candidate. This is probably due to the fact that recruiters are better with candidates than your average teammate. The reason for the teammate is that you want someone from the actual team so that when the candidate is making a decision, they already have bonded with a teammate. This is primarily triggered by the selected employee being authentic with the candidate. Then, when the candidate is going from interview to interview, that person on the team can chat with them about each interview and make sure that they have everything they need. Sort of a like an insider to the company. When the onsite interview is done, the candidate is walked outside by this chosen individual and informed that they will be emailed the results later in the week.

Many companies would reject this approach because it takes valuable time that the selected employee could have been working with a candidate that is questionable. What is often overlooked in this knee jerk reaction is that, candidates will write about a company's interview process on an online forum like Glassdoor, where other future candidates will also look and *not* interview with companies that have low ratings - Almost 60%[13] of candidates look at Social Media to get a better understanding of a company. By being thoughtful of the candidate during this process, you maximize your chances of getting more candidates by having a strong Glassdoor review.

---

13   https://www.talent-works.com/2017/09/27/social-media-recruitment/

Glassdoor has emphasized the importance of transparency in the job process. Glassdoor reported in 2018 that *"we expect more employers to start embracing transparency in application processes, partly as a way to differentiate themselves in the competition for talent. After all, the technical infrastructure to allow "package-tracking"-style updates on job applications has been in place for many years at most large employers — it's just a matter of repackaging data from existing applicant tracking software and opening it up to job seekers."* Meaning that applicants' desire for transparency and for companies to be more open carries over into a desire for authentic communication about their job interview process. Eventually, we will be able to understand the internal workings of this usually cryptic process.

Note that making the onsite interview process more thoughtful does not mean that the actual interviews have to be as difficult as well. Instead, it is simply supplying a friend to the candidate to handle the stress aspects of the interview. In fact, it would be great if the selected employee would warn the candidates of the brutality of the up and coming interview to help with the process. Make it an impressionable experience that they won't forget it.

## Commitment

Hopefully, by the end of the interview process, you have found the right candidate. Until this step, you have done a considerable amount of effort early on in the interview process to build rapport with the candidate. Traditionally, most companies offer compensation and equity and benefits like health insurance, but there are other possibilities such as:

**Work From Home (WFH)**: The Bureau of Labor Statistics found that 24% of all employed people did some or all of their work at home contrasting that to 19% in 2003.[14] However, MarketWatch has estimated by 2020, 50% of the workforce will be working partially from home.[15] With this massive change oncoming, work from home has become common in job offerings. As we shift to more working remotely, the benefits of working from home will eventually lose value as a recruiting tool.

**PTO:** SHRM states that 2% of companies actually offer this which is odd because SHRM says "The benefits can be attractive. 54 percent of employers that implemented a combined PTO program said unscheduled absences dropped by up to 10 percent when they started the new policy, according to a survey by the Alexander Hamilton Institute. Four percent found that those absences dropped by more than 20 percent."

**Leadership opportunity:** Offer access to higher decision-makers. *Deloitte Global CEO, Punit Renjen, said:*

> *"There is really no secret (to success) and there surely are no shortcuts. In my case, it was a pretty simple equation: hard work + some lucky breaks + great mentors." The last of these, the positive impact of the mentor, is clearly highlighted by our findings.*

---

14 https://www.bls.gov/opub/ted/2016/24-percent-of-employed-people-did-some-or-all-of-their-work-at-home-in-2015.htm

15 https://www.marketwatch.com/video/sectorwatch/by-2020-50-of-workforce-will-be-remote-here-how/EC18E212-D8F5-493E-9602-7E5E5D980ABD.html

> *Among those who have somebody acting as their mentor, more than nine in ten describe the quality of advice (94 percent) and the level of interest shown in their development (91 percent) as "good." Among those with mentors, 83 percent are satisfied with this aspect of their working lives.'*

**Reverse mentorship:** Jack Welch, CEO of General Electric, made it mandatory for all of his directors to have a mentee and a mentor for knowledge transfer. Perish Company found a 96% retention rate with 67 millennials when reverse mentorship relationships were implemented in the company. Point being that this is tapping into the mindset of a potential candidate and increasing the likelihood of them signing with the company.

Earlier in my speaking career, I innocently told a crowd of HR attendees, that you can customize your job offers for different employees from a time off perspective. During the middle of the presentation, a gentleman in the back told me that I had made an erroneous conclusion about how HR works. It would be unfair to give one person a privilege over the rest of the employees for one customization. I bring this up often and change is met with resistance. Know that if you want to make custom decisions and offers, HR usually has to get involved so it would be a good idea to run by custom job offers first.

The point is knowing what the candidate wants. In order to know that, you need to build a strong relationship with them so they will let you know their needs. Hence, the necessity for authenticity.

As we move forward in the world, companies will need to sort through more and more candidates and be able to decipher whether or not a piece of paper is really a good fit for a company. By leveraging authenticity, you will be able to understand the needs and wants of a candidate, and also their true nature in order to see if they are a good fit for the company.

| Phase | Then | Now/Future |
|---|---|---|
| Attention | ■ Unique selling proposition was determined by copy quality in newspaper job ads, or letters.<br>■ Communication was limited to the written word.<br>■ PR campaigns were very one-sided where external employees didn't know what was truthful. | ■ Companies can communicate their message through social media.<br>■ Communication can be through video, voice, or written.<br>■ Candidates can crowd-source reviews behind company propaganda.<br>■ Videos can be mass-produced because of inexpensive quality to make.<br>■ Huge top-of-the-funnel numbers because of the ease of resume submission.<br>■ Applicant Tracking System (ATS). |
| Interest | ■ Companies are limited to phone in pre-screening interview rounds.<br>■ Companies can only interview low volume of candidates. | ■ Companies can leverage video, voice, and virtual reality in the pre-screening rounds.<br>■ Companies can leverage technology to develop optimized interview funnels by supplying online tests.<br>■ Prescreening can be delegated. |

| Phase | Then | Now/Future |
|---|---|---|
| Commitment | ■ Limited options in job offer, salary, equity. | ■ Can offer WFH and other benefits through the power of technology.<br>■ Challenges on employee retention because of ease of leaving. |

CHAPTER 5

# The Authentic Boss

*So, I might have a career in ballet*

**During the warm** summer, when San Francisco rarely gets above 85 degrees, I was walking around a small park with my boss, Jared. We were in the northern part of San Francisco, the part that was considerably nicer than the SOMA district with cleaner streets, less homelessness and a calm and relaxed atmosphere. If you read the first chapter, this was the startup that missed the Series C funding, but that part of the story had not taken place yet.

We were in our bimonthly 1v1 meeting, a time when we both would take a break to discuss how my performance was going as a software engineer. It was a time not only to review performance but to brainstorm ideas for improvement, highlight areas of success, but most importantly, for relationship building. For the 1v1 meeting, it was my preference to go on a walk than to sit in a corporate office and discuss these personal topics. I also felt that it was easier to express myself if I was walking than sitting planted on a seat.

That park that we were circling was about half a mile in circumference and about a baseball throw across. On the other side of the busy street was the world-famous dock Embarcadero of San Francisco which had plenty of restaurants and tourist attractions for miles along the sea. It was quite a beautiful place to have a meeting. How romantic.

"So, what do you want to do with your life?"

I nearly tripped over the sidewalk when Jared dropped that question in front of me. Could he have asked me a more loaded question? Does he know what I am up to? Is this an easy way for him to segue into my side business? I had to come up with something quick that would resonate with him and be conducive to the company's goals and objectives. Should I tell him and beat him to the punch? Or should I just tell him that I wanted to continue my software engineering path to become a senior software engineer? At the time, I was starting my own consulting business and I was in the process of writing my first book. Traditionally, managers don't care what you want to do with your life, they just care if you are getting the job done. I had a few paranoid thoughts that maybe the IT department had put a bug in my computer to track every website that I have been on and he already figured out what I was up to.

"Even if you wanted to do ballet, we would support you."

Thanks Dad, I thought.

"One of the most important things for me managing you, is ensuring that you are happy with what you are doing with your life. That means even if it does not align with what you do here, we want you to be happy, so I will support you in it."

Is this a trap or is this for real? I would believe him more if he told me he was pregnant than I could say whatever I wanted to him and I would not get fired for it. How could that be possible? So, you know what I did, I lied. Flat out, I told him my dream was to be a senior software engineer and lead a large project. The most canned answer you could possibly come up without sounding like a politician.

After our walk, I couldn't get the concept out of my head that he would support me in anything I do even if I wanted to become a ballet dancer. That was even more supportive than my own parents who said they would support me in anything that does not embarrass them. As I dove into this concept more deeply, I realized there was a change that was happening in the workplace. A sort of method to effectively retain an employee and keep them happy which involved understanding how they worked on a deep psychological level. It was a way of finding what their deepest values and goals were and assisting them on their personal life journey. This new approach to me changed my perspective about how a manager conducts themselves which brings forth a new type of boss in the workplace — the authentic boss.

## The Most Optimal Team

To address the enormous amount of turnover in today's workforce, new types of management have emerged. Jared's use of this new management technique could have worked effectively if I had that authentic connection with my boss at the time; in other words, if I trusted him. If the trust had been there, I probably would have opened up to him about my real intentions about my career. Oddly enough, after the company collapsed and he found out about my business, he didn't really seem to mind. Has this new approach really been studied, analyzed and what styles of management works the best in today's workplace? The answer to the first part of that question is yes. In fact, Google did two worldwide studies, one called Project Aristotle, which focused on what elements are needed to make a great team, and the second, Project Oxygen, focused on what elements are needed for a great manager. Because Project Aristotle data depended on Project Oxygen, understanding Project Oxygen is a good first step to uncovering what makes for the optimal type of manager of today's workplace.

## Project Oxygen

In this research project done in 2008, the Google research team started with the basic question: are managers really necessary in the workplace? They developed a hypothesis based on an early belief held by some of Google's leaders and engineers that managers are, at best, a necessary evil, and at worst, a layer of bureaucracy. From here, the researchers tried to prove the premise: that managers actually *don't* matter, that the quality of a manager *didn't* impact a team's performance. The team defined a manager's quality based on two quantitative measures: manager performance ratings and manager feedback from Google's annual employee survey. After spending a good amount of time collecting and normalizing the data, the researchers discovered that managers did matter: teams with great managers were happier and more productive.

But knowing that managers did matter in the workplace did not explain what made managers great. So, the team followed up on this research and asked employees specific questions about their managers to reveal their most desirable qualities. By going through the comments from the annual employee survey and performance evaluations, the team found ten common behaviors shared by high-scoring managers. The researchers also conducted double-blind interviews with a group of the best and worst managers to find illustrative examples that demonstrated the differences between manager quality.

The qualities that the researchers found for good managers in Project Oxygen are as follows:

1. Is a good coach.
2. Empowers their team and does not micromanage.
3. Fosters an inclusive team environment.
4. Is productive, result-oriented.
5. Good communicator — listens.
6. Supports career development and gives feedback on performance.
7. Has a clear vision/strategy.
8. Has technical keys to advise the team.
9. Cross-team collaborator.
10. Is a strong decision-maker.

I analyzed this top ten list by putting them into buckets regarding their importance for authenticity in management. By sorting the qualities, what is discovered is that there is more of a need for authentic behavior in the workplace than non-authentic actions.

| Non-Authenticity Need | Authenticity Needed |
|---|---|
| 4) Productive, result-oriented. 8) Technical Keys to advise the team. 10) Strong decision-maker. | 1) Is a good coach. 2) Empower team, does not micro-manage. 3) Inclusive team environment. 5) Good communicator — listens. 6) Supports career development, gives feedback. 7) Clear Vision/strategy. 9) Cross-team collaborator. |

Juxtaposing these results to previous management styles, which usually consisted of little feedback beyond annual reviews and "Top Down" leadership approach, there seems to have been a dramatic shift in workplace management styles. In addition to what was found in Project Oxygen, managers are less used to being a resource of knowledge due to the widespread information of the internet. Hence management is more focused on personal relationship building than communicating essential knowledge for future career growth.

Looking historically at corporate managers, Peter Drucker, one of the most influential writers in the space of corporate structure and management, stated in the 1950s that the top elements of a high-performing manager consisted of: setting objectives, being able to organize, being able to motivate and communicate, measure accomplishment, and develop people. While contrasting this to what was found in the Google research, all qualities that Peter Drucker mentioned seem to resonate, but there is a further emphasis today on inclusive team environments. Building an inclusive environment depends heavily on a manager's ability to build a trustworthy relationship requiring a foundation of authenticity to be present.

To understand this shift in management, elements such as being a good coach and building an inclusive workplace environment were not common buzzwords or practices in the earlier part of the century. People now seem to be leaning more toward a work environment that values connection more than execution. To say this is a good or bad thing is hard to tell and may depend on who is asked: employer or employee. However, there is a prevalent trend that human connection is being increasingly desired from managers instead of the previous main principles of execution and setting objectives. However, contrary to this traditional structure of management, Thunderbird School of Management[16] reflected on Drucker's perspective as follows:

"Respect for the worker. Drucker believed that employees are assets not liabilities. He taught that knowledgeable workers are the essential ingredients of the modern economy, and that a hybrid management model is the sole method of demonstrating an employee's value to the organization. Central to this philosophy is the view that people are an

---

16  https://thunderbird.asu.edu/Knowledge-network/the-wisest-philosopher-in-business

organization's most valuable resource, and that a manager's job is both to prepare people to perform and give them freedom to do so."

Drucker appears to be ahead of his time with his vision of a workplace where people are the first priority, a workplace where people value authenticity. Both the ability to coach employees effectively and empower them are both vital attributes of authenticity.

## Project Aristotle

While Project Oxygen focused on what key elements make a great manager, Project Aristotle research in 2012 built upon the previous research by answering a bigger question in the minds of the researchers: what elements were needed for a strong team?

Project Aristotle was conducted in a similar style, with companywide surveys and analysis. From the data, they were able to derive five main pillars that were necessary to build a strong team:

1. **Psychological Safety:** "A belief that a team is safe for risk taking in the face of being seen as ignorant, incompetent, negative, or disruptive. In a team with high psychological safety, teammates feel safe to take risks around their team members. They feel confident that no one on the team will embarrass or punish anyone else for admitting a mistake, asking a question, or offering a new idea."

2. **Dependability:** Members consistently complete quality work on time invoking a trust among team members leading to internal dependability.

3. **Clarity and Structure:** Goals are set both at the individual or group level, and must be specific, challenging, and attainable. Google often uses Objectives and Key Results (OKRs)[17] to help set and communicate short- and long-term goals.

4. **Impact** "The results of one's work, the subjective judgement that your work is making a difference, is important for teams. Seeing that one's work is contributing to the organization's goals can help reveal impact." This is also an item that attracts top talent to companies, which we covered back in the recruitment chapter.

5. **Meaning:** Finding a sense of purpose in either the work itself or the output is important for team effectiveness. The meaning of work is personal and can vary: financial security, supporting family, helping the team succeed, or self-expression for each individual.

Again, we are seeing a trend involving authenticity, the top item, psychological safety, can be correlated with a manager's ability to be authentic by establishing trust. In addition, number three can also support the need for this item through the dimensions of attunement and vulnerability. For instance, an authentic manager can bring clarity to the expectations of the workplace if they are clear and open

---

17  https://rework.withgoogle.com/guides/set-goals-with-okrs/steps/introduction/

about how they feel about the progress and each person's participation in that journey.

## A Soft Spot?

Invariably, when authenticity is attributed to the style of the workplace management, people tend to assume that it means that a manager will be a sort of "pushover" type of personality. While this may seem true, a manager can be tough and stern while being authentic at the same time. A strict manager can establish hard deadlines, but be congruent with them, empathetic and vulnerable at the same time.

For instance, these effective team pillars can also be applied to intense environments such as the military. In the military, the overarching format is to psychologically break down candidates, take the select few who stay in and then psychologically/physically build the surviving candidates back up into soldiers. During this process, they will be put through grueling circumstances due to the severity of their work, but also be given leadership tools to help them navigate the most futile situations. On the surface, the military style may seem quite contrary to its sister corporate counterpart, but there is immense similarity between the two. The meaning and impact can be immediately applied to the sovereignty of the work that is being done. Dependability, to make sure that the teammates around each individual is strong. Clarity and Structure does not need an explanation in the context of the military. However, psychological safety does not play as a strong role here. Since the stakes are higher, being death, if there is a mistake, experimentation with failures needs to be minimized. Outside of the first pillar, the military and Google work environment share commonalities to building effective teams.

## Management Coaching With Authenticity

As seen in Project Oxygen, having a manager as a good coach is one of the most desired attributes. Even in the earlier days of Peter Drucker, it was thought that managers should develop their employees to maximize their potential and treat them as assets and not liabilities. This requires a manager to understand their employee on a deeper level involving where the employee wants to go as an individual, but also as a professional, and help them get to that point.

What is a bit startling about these commonly talked about aspects of management coaching is that, according to the *Harvard Business Review*, one of the top things that millennials look for in an occupation is being coached in their profession.[18] In addition, according to Human Capital Institute, coaching an employee can increase and drive engagement.[19] These two elements imply that old techniques of management need to be rekindled because the workers want elements such as coaching to become more commonplace and not a rare management benefit. Leveraging authenticity to find where a candidate wants to go and then coaching them to get there not only is a great tool for developing talent, but an incredible way to maximize an employee's tenure.

---

18   https://hbr.org/2015/02/millennials-want-to-be-coached-at-work

19   http://www.hci.org/lib/building-coaching-culture-increased-employee-engagement

## Technologification

Around the world, innovations are attempting to replace inefficiencies in the workplace with more optimized solutions. For management, many SaaS (Software as a Service) tools have been created to simplify everyday workplace complexities such as tracking work to employee productivity. However, how many tools can you use to increase psychological safety, instill impact or meaning to our lives when working on teams? Very few, though there have been quite a few attempts. Inevitably, humans look for traits in the workplace that cannot be optimized by technology. Meaning that the future of the workplace will still continue to need the human attributes of authenticity, Technology will complement, but not replace the need for human contact.

For a manager, one of the most difficult parts of building a team is making sure that there is cohesion, especially when the backgrounds of the individuals are diverse. Each person is working for a different reason and has a different expectation in the workplace. As a manager, the question arises of how to direct the team's efforts in the right direction with this large amount of diversity. To handle this workplace complexity, managers can leverage authenticity and also follow three steps to building a stronger team: align, build, and communicate.

## Align a Team

One of the biggest issues that arises in the workplace is when employees have different expectations. This can be demonstrated through the *Saturday Night Live* skit of a group of millennials starting to work in Corporate America.

Throughout the skit, issues such as the bean bag culture arise along with the millennials wanting to rise to the top of the ladder after only three days of work. More senior managers were disgruntled by the lack of understanding the millennials had of the workplace and they perceived the millennials to be extremely out of touch. At the end of the day, this came down to the difference of expectations in the workplace, which brings up the question: what is one of the best ways of handling these differences? You guessed it, authenticity.

As different groups of individuals go through different circumstances in the world, their understanding of how it operates can vary widely, creating issues in the workplace about work ethic, working hours, and culture. Two intertwined issues on this front, work ethic and time at work, can be related to technological changes in the world, and our ever-increasing ability to work whenever we what, wherever we want. A manager who does not learn how to build a workplace environment where people agree on things such as work ethic invites the Adam Equity Theory to take hold.

In this theory, each individual person has a number of units in their mind that is directly correlated with the amount of work that they do. For instance, for shoveling snow for 10 hours you get paid $100. If that equity is established for a particular occupation and a new employee joins, slacks off and gets paid the same $100 but for only working 5 hours, what will happen to the person who is working 10 hours for $100? The answer to that is Adam's Equity Theory will take hold. People naturally try and keep a homoeostasis in equity in work ethic. When that imbalance is noticed, the person who feels taken advantage of will attempt to correct that imbalance by changing the equity ratio in some way. Relating this back to work ethic and work-life balance, if someone who is more used to a work-from-home culture works with people who are not, that will naturally create a large amount of tension in the workplace, which will inevitably need to assimilate one of the two poles and come to an agreement.

As many companies make this shift from having people work in-house to partially remote, as in, working from home 1-2 days a week, a natural tension arises because people question whether the people working remotely are actually performing their activities on time. Again, managers will need to make an adjustment, shifting from "FaceTime Management" to "Performance Driven Management." FaceTime Management assumes that if I can see you, you must be working, while Performance Driven Management evaluates employee performance against metrics and deadlines, removing the need to see someone face-to-face to ensure that they are managed. Instead, they will be able to work remotely because deadlines and expectations are agreed upon between the manager and the employee. However, a manager will need to develop an authentic relationship with their directs to figure out if the estimations and workload are sufficient for their team.

Companies have usually solved these sorts of problems by shifting to certain types of workflows such as the Agile Model. This model leverages evaluating work and committing to work against a specific time frame, traditionally done in 2-week cycles. These cycles involve planning, estimations and retrospective. With this format, the team is able to be measured against specific timelines while also having the work allocated and agreed upon with their manager. The ability of the managers and team's ability to scope and estimate work will determine how well these workflow models can work.

Competing with the view of Performance Driven Management, Amazon uses a stronger focus on the Facetime Model along with other major companies, going so far as to time the amount of time an employee works in their seats. These major companies have started to use technology solutions such a Sociometric Solutions[20], a hardware company that has built devices that track every moment that an employee spends in the workplace in order to determine if they are being productive. Originally, it was a project developed by students at MIT to determine what made workplaces and teams like Google so efficient. Companies like Bank of America have jumped on this bandwagon attempting to test their call center efficiencies. Ben Waber, the president of Sociometrics and one of the company's founders, concluded that "In the U.S., there's this notion that your most productive time is when you're sitting at your desk staring at the computer," and what we are finding is that's not necessarily true.

In companies that are both intense but also utilizing work-from-home privileges, such as some client/consultant companies like Boston Consulting Group, have used

---

20    https://www.businessinsider.com/tracking-employees-with-productivity-sensors-2013-3

a rotational model, in which people can be online in order to address clients. Leslie Perlow, in her book *Sleeping With Your Smartphone,* analyzed how rotational work from home can influence productivity and alleviate burnout in the workplace. In her research, she found that employees were able to limit the amount of burnout by having dead time where they were not allowed to be on their phones and could work late at night. While this was effective, there were occasional exemptions that tended to intrude on the rejuvenating *unplug* time.

Whatever model you choose to leverage, keeping an eye on workers expectations and making sure your team is on the same page is important to ensure that Adam's Equity Theory does not take hold. If a manager fails to act in the integration of this theory, they will inevitably find cultural clashes developing and people consequently leaving.

## Using Authenticity with Remote Teams

Having built two companies that were entirely remote, I have seen my fair share of remote team blunders when it came to aligning workplace expectations. My favorite ones also tend to be the ones where you think you have created perfect documentation for a remote employee. After the project is completed, everything is done wrong and, when you look over the instructions, you find out that the remote person did exactly what you said, but, you were the one who wrote the instructions haphazardly.

Traditionally, remote teams are thought of to be people who will complete work without any need for human connection, or at least that is what I thought initially. However, as I became more proficient at building teams with multiple hierarchies, I realized that the human connection was extremely important and vital for a culture to exist just beyond myself. For people who are struggling with managing remote teams, being able to jump on a video and be authentic with team members is vital for retention. But more importantly, you must understand who you are working with. The two major struggles that managers will run up against when building remote teams are culture and productivity.

While productivity is much easier to measure through performance driven management, building that culture is even more important. If you have ever worked remotely for a company, it is an immensely lonely occupation. Learning how to invoke connection with your remote team members is vital to ensuring that retention is strong.

Whether HR is involved or not, each team and subgroup has its own values and beliefs, essentially a culture. While we will be exploring this more in the Authentic Leadership chapter, the key lies in making sure that your culture maintains your values when new people come on board. However, the difficult part of this is to ensure that your team's values are understood. What is odd about this is that they are implicit, not explicit, so it will take some thought. Higher-level values such as dress code and hours of labor are the most explicit and easier to align with new employees. However, other items, such as cross-team communication and off hours questions may need more thought in order to make it work.

## Build a Strong Team Foundation

After the team is effectively aligned on expectations and priorities, learning how to build relationships horizontally is the next step in building an authentic workplace. In a traditional setting, management and employee relationships are typically vertical, meaning the relationship is between the manager and the employee, up and down the workplace hierarchy. The goal is to go from vertical to horizontal with relationships between different people on the team. This brings us to the two variations to that strengthen the foundation of a team — individual and inter-team relationships.

For the individual, as previously mentioned, a manager needs to have a strong authentic relationship for a direct employee to communicate with their manager where they want to go in their career. Both require an enormous amount of empathy, or rather Attunement by the manager. The individual technique is leveraged on helping the individual grow in their career, consequentially strengthening the team. Building a strong authentic relationship with a direct may not be something that can be cultivated in a few weeks and may take months or years to build. As mentioned with Project Oxygen, one of the most important things that a manager should do is be a good coach. This means being able to help their directs navigate their career path. *Harvard Business Review* found that millennials value growth in a profession more than any other aspect, implying that they want a manager to coach them on a career path. Traditionally, this will be a career path within the company itself. However, that might not always be the case. Learning what an employee wants and helping them get there is a viable skill, even though it might not be immediately valuable to the company.

However, what is fairly interesting about this new shift in management towards coaching is that information is more available now than ever before, which devalues the knowledge of a manager. Yet, coaching remains one of the most important things that a manager can do in the workplace. Thanks to the Internet, people can jump on free websites like YouTube and online learning platforms to learn the skills to get them to the next career path level. Farther into the future, informational resources will become even more accessible, making it easier to connect with once-unreachable people. This should replace the need for career-path coaching, given that coaching is usually a knowledge transfer relationship. However, this might not be surprising when considering professional athletes when the how-to-do certain things in their sports is more available than ever, and yet, they all have coaching. Hence, the need for that human connnetion is irreplacable.

Peter Drucker pointed out in the 1950s that there will be a '"shift to a knowledge society." Managers now need to point out holes in the employee's skills set and lay out a path for them to gain those skills to help them reach their idealized self. This can be simply done by figuring out an employee's point B, finding their main limiting skill, and building a learning path around that weakness to help them. Again, this is centered around the relationship that the manager has with the employee, adding emphasis to the importance of authenticity. All things considered, the ability to strengthen the individual is the first variation of building a strong team.

Moving away from strengthening the individual and on to the team dynamic, the inter-relationships between team members is usually strengthened by subjecting a team to pressure to create a sense of reliance and interdependence.

When considering how to strengthen the inter-team bonds, an important study to look at was conducted by Thomas F. Pettigrew PhD and Linda R. Tropp in their book, *When Groups Meet*. The authors wanted to discover what conditions needed to be present when different groups meet. The analysis consisted of 515 studies including 713 independent samples, spanning the years of 1940 to 2000, involving more than a quarter million participants from 38 countries. Pettigrew and Tropp found that '94% of the studies revealed an inverse relationship between intergroup contact and prejudice." Meaning that, as the workplace becomes a more ethnically diverse place, in order for workplace cohesion to exist, elements such as emotional bonds or at least mutually understanding, need to manifest.

Interestingly enough, this not only applies to culture and ethnicity, but also to age groups, which is what I am usually focused on when working with different companies. However, if you reflect on the question of whether emotional content really helps with different groups in the workplace, it's important to note that, in order to increase cohesion between groups, or how Pettigrew and Tropp framed it as "solving intergroup conflict" you must rely on the Allport Conditions. These conditions were originally proposed by Gordon Allport' in 1954 and focus on several conditions that should be in place for different groups to work effectively. These conditions were divided as follows:

1. **Equal Status between the groups:** Ensuring that each party or group is on a level status playing field. In the corporate world, there needs to be no hierarchy within the group. One way to develop a "leveled" situation is to form an outside workplace arrangement where the parties are level.

2. **Common Goals:** The groups need to work toward a common goal, such as an annual quarterly goal or a team group of client satisfaction.

3. **Cooperation:** The group needs to work in cooperation, not competitively. A simple example would be a top performer who gets a vacation getaway rather than the best team. By having a diverse team, the team will need to depend on one another to overcome those barriers.

4. **Institutional Support:** The organization is able to support the interaction so if something goes awry, they are still able to remedy the issue.

Now that we have the Allport Conditions, you will probably be able to spot quite a few instances in the workplace where these conditions are present. Below are a few ways that companies are strengthening relationships on teams.

## Volunteering Time Off (VTO)

Volunteering time off is when employees are paid to take time off to volunteer in the community. This particular technique actually works in a multitude of ways to not only overcome barriers but also benefit the company. For starters, VTO can work as a good public relations move to show that company cares about the community. In terms of strengthening of the team, *Fortune* and research companies such as Project ROI found that VTO policies aid employee-retention efforts, which can correlate with having those bonds strengthened between team members.

When considering the Allport Conditions and how they are applied in this workplace situation, we can see that all four conditions are being met:

- **Equal Status:** Everyone is on an equal playing field when out of the office.

- **Common Goals:** The goal is to jointly volunteer together.

- **Cooperation:** No one wins something; it is the group that wins.

- **Institutional Support:** If something goes wrong, the volunteering group can help.

There are various companies that leverage the power of VTO such as SalesForce, 56 hours paid time off,[21] NuStar Energy, 72 hours paid time off,[22] and Novo Dordisk, 80 hours paid

---

21 https://www.getsalesforcebenefits.com/en/your-benefits/work-life/time-off-and-leaves

22 http://fortune.com/2016/03/21/companies-that-offer-paid-time-off-to-volunteer/

time off.[23] However, in order for the team building effects to take place with VTO, companies must be willing to have entire teams go through VTO. Unfortunately, VTO is usually an afterthought for many companies, but if companies do prioritize this strategy, they can expect to see the bonds of the team members strengthened, fortifying performance, retention, and creating an environment where the corporate facade is pulled back.

## Reverse Mentorship

Originally popularized by Jack Welch, reverse mentorship is a strategy that involves a younger employee mentoring a more seasoned leader about recent changes in the current world, usually in technology. In exchange, the leader mentors the less-seasoned employee in leadership and receives insightful questions. In a television interview, Welch, one of the most successful CEOs in corporate history, disclosed that, after hearing this technique of Reverse Mentorship, he required all of his executives to find a potential mentor within the 72 hours. His main concern was not "as executives we are not up to speed," meaning that there are various things happening in the industry that executives might not have their ear attuned to, while a younger cohort of the workforce does. An executive's experience and ability to execute, coupled with the knowledge of younger employees, can leverage the background and execute on new ideas to stay up to speed in the ever-changing world.

---

23  http://fortune.com/2016/03/21/companies-that-offer-paid-time-off-to-volunteer/

In addition to the one-on-one mentoring relationship model, organizations such as the Air Force use reverse mentoring to help stay abreast of what candidates are looking for in work. In order to gain insight on difficult questions such as what the younger workforce is looking for in a job, the Air Force assembled a panel of less-seasoned officers and asked them questions. By opening up the door and creating an environment where younger employees can speak up openly about issues, organizations can acquire valuable information that they would otherwise be hard pressed to find. The Air Force has found this to be an invaluable tool to keep up to date in the world of change.

Along with being a great tool for knowledge transfer, reverse mentorships extend to strengthen workplace relations and increase retention. Again, this feeds into authenticity in the area of attunement because an understanding of each other's reality is imperative for a mentoring relationship. Stereotyping and being rash will destroy the relationship and inhibit knowledge transfer.

Now focusing in on the Allport conditions, we find that all four stages are being met:

- **Equal Status:** Hierarchy is flipped, as both are exchanging information on an equal footing.

- **Common Goals:** Information is exchanged to help improve the state of each person's career.

- **Cooperation:** There is no other way, otherwise a relationship would not exist.

- **Institutional Support:** Human Resources is available to help if anything goes astray.

Along with all of the Allport Conditions being met, many companies currently use reverse mentoring such as Target, which brought in younger talent to help with social media, and GE, where Jack Welch popularized the idea, and United Healthcare. Unfortunately, The Delphi Group surveyed 600 companies and found that 56% of companies use mentoring relationships and only 13% use reverse mentoring. That a markedly small percent given the immense power that this mentoring strategy holds as a strategy that not only helps strengthen teams, but also doubles as a tool to keep up in the world of change.

## Offsite Retreats/Events

Can you remember back to when you were in elementary school and you saw one of your teacher outside of the classroom for the first time? In that moment, something truly amazing probably happened. If you were anything like me, when I saw my teacher, I realized they existed outside of the reality of the classroom. That they were a living, breathing, human being with values just like me. Empathy and understanding was invoked simply by seeing them in another environment, one where they were no longer my teacher, but another person in the world.

When companies arrange offsite events, on the surface level, it's about having employees have some fun outside of the office as a reward. This usually happens when a goal is completed where having the team participate in something offsite serves as a mass escape. Additionally, it helps with building stronger relationships and rewarding employees for their hard performance. However, these subtle actions go a long way in strengthening relationships in the workplace. In the paradigm of authenticity, you will see that Congruence is being addressed here. People are able to strip back the corporate facade and have a more connected relationship. Interestingly, by interacting on a deeper level with one another, they are able to learn to trust each other on a deeper level.

As we review the Allport conditions, we find they are again met with Offsite Retreats:

- **Equal Status**: Ensuring that everyone is equal in the events, managers are not able to order their directs around.
- **Common goals:** They must complete a task to accomplish the award together.
- **Cooperation:** They must cooperate in order to win.
- **Institutional Support:** Staff onsite to help with any conflicts.

Some companies that are using this strategy: Dropbox, Amazon and Lithium Technologies.

When you are able to create Allport conditions within the workplace, you will find it easier to increase team cohesion and grow the bonds within the team. However, Pettigrew and Tropp found that each group is usually anxious and uncomfortable at first. The authors divide this into three different variables: intergroup knowledge, anxiety and empathy. By providing useful information to the group about the outgroup, anxiety is reduced in intergroup encounters. The authors found that continuous mediation through anxiety reduction tended to help with the contact's effects on prejudice. (Pg 81). In addition, empathy was also used to "conscious and non-conscious outgroup stereotyping as well as increase the overlap between representations of the self and the outgroup."

I hope these techniques help you build stronger teams in the workplace where people are excited about coming to work. These are very common and relatively straightforward, but they all work in great ways to not only build stronger relationships between team members but also to create a more authentic workplace.

# Communication

Once you are able to strengthen your team's relationships, you will end up finding that both the individual and the team will be moving effectively, but this will require some form of feedback in times when the team gets off track. On the individual level, a common method to deliver feedback is the "360 review." These were one of the earliest recorded uses of surveys to gather information about employees starting in the 1950s. These surveys usually consisted of each person being evaluated by their coworkers grading the evaluated person's performance. The average of this feedback would be the score of the employee. However, more recently, there have been increasing demands for more consistent feedback than a 360 review, according to the news outlet Muse[24]. This shift should not come as a surprise; people are naturally goal-seeking and long for consistent

---

24   https://www.themuse.com/advice/what-millennials-really-need-hint-its-not-feedback

feedback which increases the chance of the hitting a goal. Feedback should be measured and kept transparent. While difficult, this is very useful from an esteem perspective for the employee, but also the manager as well by being able to measure progress.

Even though the 360 review is widely used, it is also widely criticized because "Many 360-degree feedback tools are not customized to the needs of the organizations in which they are used.[5] 360-degree feedback is not equally useful in all types of organizations and with all types of jobs. Additionally, using 360-degree feedback tools for appraisal purposes has increasingly come under fire as performance criteria may not be valid and job-based, employees may not be adequately trained to evaluate a co-worker's performance, and feedback providers can manipulate these systems.[9] Employee manipulation of feedback ratings has been reported in some companies using 360-degree feedback for performance evaluation including GE (Welch 2001), IBM (Linman 2011), and Amazon (Kantor and Streitfeld 2015)." Hence it would probably be best to include more consistent feedback for the individual. In other words, keeping it more transparent.

In the *One Minute Manager,* Kenneth H. Blanchard and Spencer Johnson discuss a very simple way of giving feedback. The theory is to break apart the negative and positive feedback and simply give it in one-minute periods. That way, when a larger review comes about, the employee already has a strong understanding of where they tilt the scale. However, the ability for a manager to give constructive feedback is really where things get tricky. Very often, managers avoid giving feedback in order to avoid conflict. However, it's how you give the feedback that is important. This flies right in the face of the sandwich technique that is often used to give and receive feedback.

Another way of delivering feedback can be viewed through the filter of Non-Violent Communication, originally coined by Rosenberg. This particular method has four phases- observations, feelings, needs and requests. Here is where it ties back into authenticity. Attunement is used to observe and empathetically understand what has actually happened, then establishing how you feel about the event. This is covering the attunement phase, then expressing your needs to feel safe and lastly the request, or rather the part of negative feedback. Here is a simple example:

"Felix, when I (1) see socks under the coffee table I (2) feel irritated because I am needing (3) more order in the room that we share in common. (4) Would you be willing to put your socks in your room or in the washing machine? [If the response lacks clarity or seems disconnected, then request feedback.] (5) So, I know that you understood me, would you tell me what you heard me say?" The point is expressing yourself in this feedback style will be much more effective in getting the results you want from a coworker.

## Communication From the Team

While you may communicate feedback to your team, there is also the flip side, which is receiving feedback from the team. At one time or another, someone on your team has an idea about how to make something better. As a manager, your task is to be aware of these ideas and vet them for future implementation. However, unless you have a strong relationship with those people who are contributing ideas, where they trust and feel safe, Attunement and being Vulnerable (Project Aristotle, number one effective team element), your employees will not contribute ideas. In addition, as a manager or someone who is used to a set of rules and workflow, inevitably you begin to become aware of certain flaws and errors in the model. Hence, when you have a team that is contributing ideas, they will be able to diagnosis and bring to your attention things that need fixing.

When you are able to leverage the knowledge of a team, a collaboration model emerges instead of a dictatorial one, where the entity is both a part of the individual and the manager. However, as wonderful as this may seem, managers must be able to set the tone of the workplace environment where people feel comfortable enough to bring forth ideas. Even in the best of companies, take Facebook, an employee left and created WhatsApp that Facebook later needed to acquire for $19 billion. What if Facebook was able to harness this idea?

There are various companies that are aware of this issue and develop internal incubators to fund startup ideas and harness feedback/ideas from employees internally, including large companies such as Coca Cola, Mastercard, General Electric, IBM. "They're holding innovation contests and using panels of executives to dole out investment dollars to fund internal startup ideas," according to Jennifer Alsever[25]

---

25  http://fortune.com/2015/04/26/startups-inside-giant-companies/

a *Forbes* contributor and journalist. These innovative contests are referred to as Hackathons, were employees can experiment and build something within a short period of time, usually 24-72 hours, and produce a business to solve a problem. Hackathons are rapidly growing in popularity not only in the tech world. The crux of the notion can also be used as external events aimed at enhancing a firm's reputation in the eyes of software developers. Indeed, some firms consider hackathons as essentially good PR, and pay for them out of their marketing budgets, according to *The Economist*. Websites like mlh.io list all of the public available hackathons in the United States, occasionally four a day.

One of the most famous examples of a hackathon occurred back in 2010 when Jared Hecht and Steve Martocci had an idea on how to transform instant messaging communication. In order to do this, they decided to join the TechCrunch Disrupt 2010 hackathon. During this hackathon, they built a rough prototype of GroupMe. GroupMe works by downloading an app or allowing access to the service online, with a user forming an account by providing a name, cell phone number and a password, or by connecting through a Facebook or Twitter account. The service then syncs with the user's contacts and from that point forward the user can make messaging groups of any size.

They took this idea, raised funding and, within a few months, attracted $10.6 million in venture capital from Khosla Ventures, General Catalyst Partners, angel investors, and others. Excited by this early momentum, they continued building out the app until, 16 months after the initial idea, they were acquired by Skype for $80.6 million. As much as this seems like a fairy tale, and it is pretty much as close as it gets to one, many companies today are founded and built in this style.

The whole point of introducing that story is to show you the potential of having a group of individuals build out their ideas in a controlled setting, and then release it to the world. Every person has the ability to produce ideas. The only question then is, as a manager, would you have the ability to harness this creativity to maximize the creator's potential and also have it benefit the company?

While hackathons may be a companywide effort, there are many small things that managers can do to increase the likelihood that someone will have their ideas heard. Here is a small list:

- Employee ideas.
- Implementation.
- Given authority.
- More engagement.
- Better employee morale.

The goal here is to harness the new ideas that employees have. Between 1 and 2 comes the vetting phase. Managers here will typically face the best opportunity to either build or destroy the employee's ambitions. It can be like a young child painting for the first time and showing a parent their marvelous creation. Chances are, it will be difficult to interpret what the child actually drew because it was their first drawing. If the parent is stern and rejects the drawing, the child is more likely to avoid showing the parent and all together not paint in general.[26] The same could be said for the workplace: a new employee has a great idea that they want to introduce to their boss, which more likely than not, has already been thought of. Still, the employee puts the manager on the spot on whether or not they are going to encourage or discourage their direct. Using authenticity here is extremely important to ensure that an employee walks away with or without ownership of the project, on point and understanding of the situation.

In fact, taking a closer look at the impact of ownership and employee productivity, in the *National Bureau of Economic Research,* David R Francis summarizes research done that involved having employees have more ownership over projects. The surprising finding was that it did not increase employee productivity, but "This supports the idea that it is not ownership per se, but the cooperative culture that can be fostered by employee ownership, that drives better workplace performance in ESOP firms." An interesting finding that could be attested to the fact that people like having control over what they do. From the communication side of things, it is important to ensure that your communication with your employees leverages authenticity and also harnesses their ideas through the same medium.

---

26  https://www.apa.org/education/ce/psychology-encouragement.pdf

# Managing Office Politics Through Authenticity

Initially, I was not planning on involving politics in this book, however, I thought it would be necessary in order to define authenticity in the workplace. For that purpose, I will approach the topic of politics by discussing how to build cohesion in the workplace of today, which is filled with different political beliefs. In management, external politics have a strong chance of coming up in the workplace and you need to have the ability to approach it effectively in order to maintain workplace cohesion.

Metaphorically, politics can be thought of as a game of soccer that is being played in the middle of a courtyard. Imagine that you were at one corner of the courtyard and you had to venture to the other side because there was a grocery store enticing enough to make you want to walk over there. As you would walk across the courtyard, you would see the group of individuals playing the game of soccer. Then, you are faced with different choices, you could watch in entertainment, join in, or walk around the game, hoping you won't interfere in any way. If you were to try and avoid the game, there is still a possibility that you will get hit with the soccer ball or a player would run into without you seeing them. Lastly, you can join in, and learn the rules and to keep up with the flow of the game. Then, you will finally reach the other side of the courtyard, maybe or maybe not in one piece. However, inevitably you will need to get to the other side of the courtyard.

Politics is very much the same way. It exists and you can choose to watch and spectate, you can join the game, or you can try and avoid it all together, but sometimes you will get hit with it, even when you do not see it coming, Today, a lot of people are in the latter situation, especially in the workplace where politics can create heated conversations, stressful environments and very difficult workplaces. However, by learning how to use it, they can turn into powerful tool that will serve as the catalyst for a positive change.

I was very unaware of the politic scene in the workplace until I was hit in the head with the metaphorical soccer ball of politics. A few years ago, I was catching up with an old coworker who was a manager at a large tech firm. Our conversation covered what was happening over the past few years and eventually the workplace inclusion movement came up. He was describing bias training and the recent political events that were taking place at the company he worked at. While he started on a positive note, he eventually began to become paranoid, constantly looking around and wondering if someone was eavesdropping on our conversation. He began telling that while he found the training to be very informative, he feared for his current employment situation. He was extremely worried that, if he said one thing wrong, someone would take that opportunity to report it to the higher authorities, and it would get into the news and his career would be ruined in the blink of an eye.

To better understand his point of view, I will give a brief background on the friend who I was talking to. He was a past co-worker and I got to see his management style up close. I knew him intimately and he was one of the nicest people I knew, very low on disagreeableness. I will define him as someone nice, so much so that it could be to the point of being a slight pushover. He was the last person who would ever intentionally offend someone.

Reflecting on this, with the different political and social movements that are taking place in today's world, such as the inclusion movement, I believe that creates a two-sided coin. On one side, there is the awareness factor, where people who have gone through abuse are given a voice and are able to find help in difficult situations. On the other side, people start to worry about making a mistake and being put on the public shame wagon. When addressing things such as psychological safety in the workplace, making mistakes and not suffering the consequences is a part of the equation. When issues like this arise, people draw back and become reclusive. Why? Because saying something wrong at the wrong time is a lot more severe than not saying anything at all, even if you are not trying to offend someone.

Since this book is focused on leveraging authenticity in the workplace, specifically how to create a safe and effective working environment, politics needs to be addressed because that plays an enormous part of that feeling of authenticity and safety, regardless of what side of the fence you are on. An ability for a manager to address these issue head on will help.

## How the Internet Is Changing the World of Politics

The birth of the Internet, as marvelous at it was for the world, came with unexpected consequences resulting in major culture shifts. With platforms such as LinkedIn, Instagram, Facebook, and most dramatically, Twitter, the world of news and gossip can spread faster than ever before. With this supernatural affect, many people turned into celebrities overnight, while many others had their careers destroyed. For instance, Justine Sacco, a director of communications for a New York-based internet company, was on her way to Africa. Before her flight, she sent out a controversial tweet about AIDS and her immunity to the disease because she is white. During her flight, without imagining and isolated from the social media while on the air, her controversial tweet went viral in a couple of hours. When her name was queried on Google, her airplane location showed on Google Maps. By the time she landed in Africa, there was a capture order by the authorities, which resulted in her arrest and later on, her firing.

Before the internet and the creation of social media, comments such as the one made by Sacco would disappear into the bucket of unnecessary comments. Now, with social media becoming a faceless mob, no one can be sure what comments might become viral to this degree, subjecting people to punishment or contempt. In other words, with social media, anything that is said has the potential to boomerang and annihilate a person's career. Because, with the rise of different political movements, we have developed a mob mentality that threatens anyone who does not abide by its ever-changing rules.

Jaron Lanier, an author and philosopher who is considered the father of the Virtual Reality movement, cautions about the dangers that social media can bring to the world. In his critique of the collective wisdom on an article in *Edge* titled "Beware the Online Collective," Lanier reflects about this concerning reality:

> "I wonder if some aspect of human nature evolved in the context of competing packs. We might be genetically wired to be vulnerable to the lure of the mob....What's to stop an online mass of anonymous but connected people from suddenly turning into a mean mob, just like masses of people have time and time again in the history of every human culture? It's amazing that details in the design of online software can bring out such varied potentials in human behavior. It's time to think about that power on a moral basis."

While the mob is one dangerous dimension, there is also the ease of producibility which allows anyone to broadcast their opinions, fabricate "news" without checking facts, and get a large following and attention by creating "click bait" — the more controversial, the more effective tool. Although the practice of spreading of rumors has always been a favorite pastime for many, it has now been scaled up by social media. Even in the past, people would usually remember the first news story about a case, even if it was later proven that the accused party was completely innocent. Most people wouldn't make the effort to follow the story and find out the end result, which sometimes takes years in big corporate cases. It is basically a system of guilty, once accused, even if proven innocent at a later stage. The reputation of the person who is accused is forever tarnished.

On the positive side of the spectrum, social media is not part of a monopoly in place that tries to censor news. It is simply a free-for-all with no "gatekeepers." This means that fake news can be corrected and different perspectives can quickly be presented; and that journalists now have to be more careful with what they publish.

However, it also means that we can create communities around common concerns and causes by using hashtags and groups. In other words, important issues that are on the minds of the general population will be voiced and brought to the surface.

Let's take a closer look at an example, the famous #MeToo movement that I mentioned in the introductory story. According to its founder, Tarana Burke, it is about empowerment through empathy, it is about telling people who have experienced any kind of sexual violence that "you are not alone", it is about something Tarana calls "radical community," where we come together to eradicate sexual violence. There are resources offered on the website for everyone who might experience sexual violence to get help, regardless of gender, color or nationality. Even though it originally started as a movement to support "young women of color from low wealth communities," it has since expanded to be an inclusive movement for all the women in need of help.

With movements like this, an interesting dichotomy arises, on one side, the general public is able to bring issues into the light that would have never had such a powerful voice in the past. On the other, there is the danger of avoiding being falsely accused and being thrown into the faceless mob of social media. While one that cannot exist without the other, it is important to figure out how to build a work environment where people feel safe in order to strengthen the team cohesion principle.

## Developing a Workplace That Embraces Diverse Political Views

Politics in the workplace cannot be approached by isolating a person or team or by firing someone because they are not communicating in the desired way. This is a holistic issue and needs to be treated as such. By reducing politics in the workplace, we need to reduce fear and increase trust, according to Stephen M.R. Covey, author of *Speed of Trust*: "The simple, often overlooked fact is this: work gets done with and through people. There's nothing more impactful on people, their work, and their performance, than trust."

To accomplish this level of trust, there must be an effort to create collaborative environments where people are encouraged to work together, to complement each other, to be open and honest about what they can and can't do. HR plays a major role in this process, but it cannot operate in isolation. Trust and openness need to be embedded in the culture. Leadership and strategy need to be aligned to the culture. It wouldn't make sense, for example, to promote a culture of collaboration and trust, while at the same time setting KPIs and goals that create internal competition. In other words, the best way to deal with politics in the workplace is to prevent the problem by anticipating it, rather than having to cope with the debris.

There are many different approaches when addressing politics in the workplace from a management perspective. In this short section, I will list a few avenues you can take to address political issues in the workplace. Hopefully you will find that one of these avenues will help in order to mitigate the tension within the team by creating the cohesion you were always looking for.

The first method, which is my preferred approach, involves not addressing it head-on but indirectly. Strengthening a team's relationships, empathy and understanding will naturally manifest causing political differences to become negligible. However, if the relationships are not strong and the contact between the groups are negative, as Thomas Pettigrew pointed out, then the differences in the groups worsen. Hence, what was mentioned previously in this chapter about different ways to strengthen the relationships of the team can help indirectly with external political issues. This approach also has the added benefit of not putting employees in situations that they don't want to be in, such as mandatory trainings. Instead, differences are understood in an organic way.

The second way of addressing diverse political views is having resources onsite that help to bringing light and understanding to the political issues at hand — the option is there but it is not mandatory. These methods can be seen as having town hall meetings about the issues or hosting workshops, where people can learn about the controversial political issues. While I think having workshops about bias training can be helpful, addressing issues at the town hall meeting level can cause a lot of friction. Often people are not willing to speak up about political issues in public and in the workplace, in fear that someone would judge them negatively.

The third option is having a mandatory approach where topics are addressed head-on by manual facilitation of hot topics in the workplace. Usually human resources or an outside consultant helps discuss these issues in the workplace. This process would involve inviting multiple people into a room to discuss a politically charged issue or recent political event. For instance, a police shooting impacting a particular demographic.

For the meeting facilitation in the book *We Can't Talk About That At Work,* the author, who specializes in facilitating difficult conversations at work, broke down the process into a 4E process goes as follows:

- **Exposure**: What is your identity, close friends, community experience — engaging with others who are cross-cultural.

- **Education**: Having a formal education in the difference between the two.

- **Empathy**: Learning to deploy empathy and learning the other people's preference for communication.

- **Experience**: Comparing your background and life experiences to the other individual

With this 4E method, people in the workplace can address issues head-on. I suggest picking up Mary-Frances Winter's book if you are curious about its applicability in the workplace.

A manager is someone who can make a working environment a hellish nightmare or a peaceful serenity. At the end of the day, we are not able to control what people think, so instead of focusing on people's political views, it would be better to concentrate on how to help people of different political beliefs work. Hopefully, through what you learned in this chapter you will be able to strengthen your employee relationships in the workplace and manage them effectively. By using these tools, you will become an Authentic Boss that will make an ever-changing positive impact.

Chapter 6

# Culture Driven Authentic Leadership

*How did you embody our company culture this past year?*

   **A.**   We Build Trust Every Day.

   **B.**   We Love to Teach and Learn.

   **C.**   We Set the Standard.

   **D.**   We Win Together.

How did I build trust every day and with who? Of course, I love to teach and learn. What is the standard and what am I comparing it to? Winning? As in, if I do well this quarter and my team doesn't, does that violate We Win Together?

It was another one of those surveys that the HR team would have each employee answer every year. For some reason, I had no idea how to answer this one. We were all emailed a survey usually by SurveyMonkey and with the fine print letters THIS IS IN COMPLETE CONFIDENTIALITY, YOUR ANSWERS WON'T BE SHARED WITH ANYONE ELSE. I actually knew this wasn't true because it was my annual review and my manager was going to need to read this over. Maybe this was a mistake, because the quarterly surveys about employee happiness were shared at the town hall meeting. During those meetings, the HR team would take sound bites from each survey, anonymously post them, then the executive team would discuss them with the entire company.

Overcoming my procrastination, I made up an answer that I thought would get me the most points by talking about how I built trust with my team by asking them for feedback on whenever I pushed code to answer- *A. We build Trust Every Day.* For *B.* I put something down about how I showed the new person around and made them feel welcome, teaching them the culture as I liked to put it. After filling out the long form questions that felt more like a SAT, than an annual review, I got up and walked around the San Francisco office to treat myself to a well-earned bathroom break.

What was annoying about these offices was that there was a bathroom at the very end of the hall. And by hall, I mean over 200 feet of hall. It was a hauling hall in its truest form. Along the hall on the left-hand side were ten-foot-tall paintings of Silicon Valley Kool Aid: a large hand with a thumbs up, an icon of a magician's hat, and a few others that could be found in a CSS Font-Awesome library (an engineering joke).

Then it clicked. I turned to look at the large icon which actually meant something relevant to my life. *These massive painted icons were the values of the company!* The survey I just filled out was actually referring to these large icons that I walked by whenever nature called. The thumbs up was for 'We Build Trust Everyday', the magician hat was for 'We Love to Teach and Learn'. Being at the company for over a year and not knowing what these large paintings meant seemed silly, but at the same time, it wasn't. I couldn't tell you how many companies I have visited either for business or eating their catered lunches when visiting friends that had the company values posted on the walls, and yet you wouldn't be able to list the values of the company if you weren't looking at them.

Traditionally, these values used to be in a framed picture next to the entrance door, but ever since the Silicon Valley interior designers became a thing, large pretty paintings were put around offices in great celebration of these once-boring pictures. So, what was the problem? I did not absorb the values; they were just there.

Painting values on a wall and expecting employees to live by them does not make any sense. It is like a parent lecturing their child on the importance of not smoking, and then lighting a cigarette after the discussion is over. The child is not going to remember the lecture; rather, it is the parent smoking the cigarette that the child will remember.

Leadership is very much the same thing in companies; it is the embodiment of these values that influences the rest of the employees in the company that inevitably creates the culture. The values are always there in a metaphysical sense, whether or not they are painted on a wall, and it is the decision of the leadership of the company to choose the values in order to determine the kind of culture that they want to manifest. In other words, one of the best ways to build a strong culture in the workplace, instead of painting icons on the walls, is through Authentic Leadership.

## Transparency in Leadership

Transparency leads to predictability and predictability leads to security, and that security gives someone a strong understanding of whether or not it is worth staying with a company. Transparency is one of the most desired attributes in the workplace because of our innate desire for security in our environment. This desire can be demonstrated through Maslow's hierarchy, where the bottom of the pyramid represents the foundation of our lives, In this bottom we see security as one of the first elements that we are motivated to master. In the workplace, this is usually referred to as financial security. The manifestation of the desire for security can be seen through many innovations and creations. One manifestation can be seen as the founding of the company Glassdoor, which was discussed earlier in this book. Ultimately, these manifestations stem from employee desires to have a better understanding of the internal working of the company, drawn from our psychological need for safety.

In this chapter, it will be worth discussing leadership and how authenticity can help with corporate transparency because of this strong desire that we have for security. Traditionally, when corporate transparency is brought to organizations, it can be implemented in a variety of different ways, usually physical. Many times, companies do not feel transparent after all of these changes are made. With that said, here are a few ways that I have seen corporate companies miss the ball when attempting to create a workplace environment that is transparent:

- **Transparent Meeting Rooms**: Yes, I actually have been given tours of companies where they claimed that the visually transparent rooms increase corporate transparency, which is true from a visual perspective. Yet, the rooms are soundproof. I am not sure that, if I can see someone talking, but not hear them, it would really help with security. Teem, a company that helps install transparent meeting rooms, claims that doing this causes the employee to be held more accountable "No one wants to be caught slacking off during an important meeting."[27]

- **Open Workspace Environments**: A concept originally popularized by Intel back in the 1990s that can completely be taken out of context, this involves workplaces removing all cubicle walls and having completely open designs. *Remote Work Will be the New Norm:* According to recent Fuze research, 83 percent of workers don't think they need to be in an office[28] to be productive, and 38 percent said they would enjoy their job more if they were allowed to work remotely. Atlassian even claimed that open workspaces help with corporate transparency, but probably forgot to add it was the visual sense not in an emotional sense.[29]

---

27  https://www.teem.com/pricing/
28  https://www.inc.com/jeremy-goldman/9-ways-to-build-the-office-of-tomorrow.html?cid=search
29  https://www.atlassian.com/blog/confluence/7-pros-and-cons-of-open-workspaces-and-how-to-compensate-for-them

- **All-hands Meeting:** A very powerful tool for communicating transparency, but also an avenue where employees get a break from where they work and drink the company Kool Aid. Sometimes providing negative feedback is helpful in these meetings.

In other words, there is no substitute for transparent leadership. Companies are similar to people in that they have a tendency to try to change their environment, rather than changing themselves. This accounts for a lot of the creative and often, ineffective ideas that usually lead to unnecessary corporate spending that can be shown in the 13% increase in interior design jobs in the next decade which AutoDesk concluded in their research.

However, if a company, leader, or individual wants to create an environment that feels transparent, safe and secure, the task will inevitably fall on the individual's own ability to cultivate attributes of transparency rather than the environment. As much as the environment may appear to be safe, the people must propagate that value of safety in the company. A definition of culture by TAMU University goes as follows: "A culture is a way of life of a group of people — the behaviors, beliefs, values, and symbols that they accept, generally without thinking about them." If the leaders don't demonstrate the values of safety, the rest of the company will struggle to absorb those values, stifling the company's atmosphere.

Culture in this respect is the unconscious set of rules that a group of people agree upon. If you really want to hurt your brain, William James said "Whenever two people meet, there are really six people present. There is each man as he sees himself, each man as the other person sees him, and each man as he really is." That thing that is formed when people meet is a part of the culture, the culture being a product of the individuals. Transparency by deduction must come from the individuals.

On the contrary, there are arguments stating that you and your environment are one and the same. As Jordan Peterson, a popular thinker and philosopher of the 21st century put it, "clean your room before you take on the world." Having the symbolic representation to clean up your area of life before you tell others to clean up theirs. When discussing this topic, Peterson often explores the phenomenon that people are often connected with their environment making them one and the same at times. While I do agree with this point, I believe that an individual attempting to create an authentic culture in the fewest of steps should opt for authenticity as a value in the individual, instead of the physical environment appearing as transparent. What I find absolutely fascinating about the concept of culture is that it is always present when there is more than one person. It is not something that is created by writing values on a wall and telling the corporation that these are the select values.

I became conscious of this concept in two ways, one when I was talking to the chief of human resources at Box Technologies and the other, in my own company. With Box, I was asking the CHRO about how they were able to create a fun-filled culture, having in the back of my mind that people all have different values, so how would this be possible? She told me it was shown through the leadership team where they would all play games; however, she quickly changed the subject thereafter. That is when I knew it wasn't the case. She wasn't explicitly clear on the company culture because that was something that was organically developed through the intrinsic values of the employees, not the values arbitarily choosen by the executive team.

In my own company, I realized this when I was talking to my team about the remote working environment we had. Trish, a manager in my company, mentioned that it was a fun place to work, and you had to get your work done on time and everything would be okay. I didn't know that was the culture of the company I built, but I knew it was a value that I held very near to me, getting work done on time and holding personal integrity to the people around you. It was an implicit value, that somehow, I impacted the culture throughout the company I was building without knowing. We never decided on values, which is why I found the vocalization so fascinating.

If a transparent culture comes from the individuals, then the leadership is a driving component, and one of the most important aspects of leadership is "embodied leadership." This is a simple concept holding that the individual must cultivate the attributes they want in the environment first in themselves, before it will manifest in their immediate environment. Meaning that, if a leader wants there to be authenticity in the workplace, it needs to start with them. However, this is a roundabout concept because instead of thinking of the actions that will need to be perceived as authentic, focusing on caring for the individuals and their safety will bring about authentic actions.

However, in today's workplace, thanks to the ever-increasing infiltration of technology, people are almost forced to become authentic. If a CEO says something that later turns out to be a lie, someone could tweet, or even write a book about an incident, or maybe go so far as to claim the lack of transparency by the company and still neglecting to say the name of the company. While this can be extremely stressful for many employees, it can also work as a benefactor where leaders are held to the integrity of the infinite history that the internet preserves.

## Top Down vs Bottom Up

So what will work better to create an authentic workplace? Expecting the leaders to become authentic [Top Down] or the rest of the employees in the company [Bottom up]? If you are not familiar with these terms, here is a simple way to look at them. Top Down is when an organization is led by the executive team, where an order is carried out through the mid-level managers and down to the entry-level workers. Bottom Up is when the company is led by the bottom level employees from a hierarchical perspective. Examples of companies that are being led from bottom up are ones that follow employee feedback in surveys, or companies that have to increase wages due to employees going on strike. While I believe both models are extremely important for an organization to function, top down is much easier to use to create companywide authenticity.

While attempting to create companywide authenticity, it is much easier for its manifestation to come from the managers and higher-up employees than from the lower level.

Traditionally, when a manager gives their direct an assignment, it is much easier for that assignment to be carried out than the reverse, which usually ends up getting the direct fired. However, there has been a definite change in that today, not necessarily from the standpoint that directs of managers will not follow orders, but rather, a more collaborative approach between manager/leader and employee. Fond[30], a company that specializes in employee benefit programs, in a recent study mentioned that "Employees today are searching for companies they can build relationships with over the long term creating a more egalitarian structure. They want management to see them as partners rather than subordinates." This implies that more of an emotional relationship is needed by managers giving more power to Bottom Up, but still pales in comparison to the power of the leaders of the company demonstrating authenticity.

While we may think that this is a new thing for building a strong relationship between superior and direct, leadership formats like this go historically all the way back to Alexander the Great. He was known to have memorized the names of his soldiers which numbered in the thousands and could recall unique details about them in order to make them feel closer and more loyal to his command. Hence, building a strong relationship with a direct employee is nothing new. What is new is that companies are starting to utilize this technique more often, leading to it becoming not an exceptional benefit in the workplace, but rather an expectation.

---

30  https://fond.co/blog/employer-employee-relationship-changed/

If a company is to be led from the Top Down, the chain of relationships must be strong from the very top CEO position, all the way down to the bottom level employee who will be carrying out the task. This is commonly referred to as the Chain of Command. There are numerous cases where companies have a breakdown in the chain of command. This usually consisted of each level somehow altering the initiative, leading to a game of telephone distorting the message further as it goes down the hierarchy.

When I was working in corporate, I had experienced a break in Chain of Command on various levels that emitted companywide dissonance and uncertainty. While this is a true story, I will avoid saying the company names in order to preserve the privacy of the company, while demonstrating the actual problem. In the past year, Company X that I was working for acquired Startup Y for over $100 million. After bringing on half of the new staff of Startup Y and firing the rest, Startup Y worked inside of Company X for about one year before anything significant happened. During that downtime, the Company X employees learned more about the "promises" that Startup Y was supposed to deliver to enhance the main product of Company X. Instead of being delighted what they found, the entry level employees realized that the product was not what they thought it was, and was actually quite inferior than the executive team originally thought.

With this skepticism in the air, when the executive team of Company X finally decided to start incorporating the new data of Startup Y, the entry level employees were reluctant to move and slow-walked the project. With optimism down, the project began to expand rapidly in size taking much more resources than the team originally anticipated causing further issues. Eventually, the entry level employees went to their manager and asked why they were spending money on something that was not promising. The manager said it was a political decision and they should go to their superior if they had issues. The same thing was relayed to the next two superiors to where the entry level employees finally reached the CTO of the company. When they sat down with the CTO and told him what they found, the CTO immediately corrected them and told them the real reason for the project. That real reason was something completely different and much more effective than the entry level employees originally thought. Unfortunately, the conversation did not go well because the employees were more aware of the problems than the CTO so they return to their work discouraged, knowing that their efforts to make a companywide change were not heard.

So how could this have been avoided in the first place? Well, there were several breakdowns:

1. The communication between the CTO and the chain of command was broken. A simple case of telephone gone wrong.

2. The chain of command at the VP level did not question what the CTO was doing and successfully dodged a political bullet in order to keep their jobs.

3. The mid-level managers also did not act to in order keep their jobs, but also wasted the company's resources through misdirection.

While difficult to grasp all of the causations of this problem. it ultimately comes down to one prominent point: The trust between the VP and the CTO was non-existent. If there was more trust, the VP could have questioned the CTO's decisions and avoided the breakdown in command.

If there was enough trust in the relationship between the manager and the direct, then the information would have been relayed and successfully avoided a miscommunication that was causing the company millions of dollars. However, because the CTO was not receptive to the group of entry level employees' perspective, he would also not be receptive to the VP had the VP challenged the CTO's initial command.

The point of this example is to demonstrate how authenticity can improve the power behind the chain of command and consequently create leadership change that resonates companywide. In addition, it is much more difficult to create bottom-up change than top-down. With this at hand, as individuals climb up the proverbial corporate hierarchy, they will be given more opportunity to exercise authenticity to ensure that the people around them trust them.

## Law of Connection

One the most important skills of a leader is knowing how to motivate people in your immediate circle, which brings us to the Law of Connection. John Maxwell, an internationally known speaker and author having sold over 13 million books, in his most popular book *The 21 Laws of Leadership*, further expands upon on the concept of authenticity in leadership in Chapter 10: The Law of Connection. More specifically, in order for people to follow, you must touch them in their hearts.

A powerful example that Maxwell emphasized in this chapter was when George W. Bush was president as the tragic September 11th terrorist attack destroyed the Twin Towers in New York. Bush had just became president and was completely taken off guard when he was told of the attack in the middle of reading to an elementary classroom filled with children. As Maxwell recounts, "The people of the United States were angry. They were fearful. They were uncertain about the future. And they were in mourning for the thousands of people who lost their lives to the terrorists."

What Bush did not foresee was that this was an amazing opportunity to utilize the Law of Connection and touch the people of the United States by being authentic in his response to the incident. A few days after the burning of the Twin Towers, Bush went to Ground Zero and addressed the mourning crowd, "The nation sends its love and compassion to everybody who's here." Eventually, people started shouting at Bush in the middle of his speech in which he retorted impromptu in an authentic way, "I can hear you. The rest of the world hears you. And the people who knocked these buildings down will hear all of us soon." While that may not have seemed like an important moment at the time, it was one of the most defying moments of Bush's presidency, when he reached out to the people, not only letting them know he could feel their pain, but also empathized with them by letting them know that he was vengeful, with "they will hear all of us soon' a perfect example of authentic leadership.

It is in these moments that many leaders are defined as individuals, when they have a small moment in time to capture the hearts of the ones they lead. These are often times of turmoil and if they respond in a way that is heartfelt, compassionate, and attuned to the follower's reality, they will have successfully utilized the Law of Connection. People are logically persuaded by facts and figures, but, ultimately, they will need to be persuaded emotionally. The ability for a leader to be true and authentic is one of the most important ways of capturing the hearts of a following and motivating them to action.

Another example of a person in power who successfully captured the hearts of a following was Jørgen Vig Knudstorp, past CEO of LEGO. Many people did not know at the time that the toy giant Lego in the early 2000s was going through some trying times that could have ultimately led to the nostalgic childhood toy being forever gone. Lego was losing roughly $1 million a day, had overextended itself into categories like branded children's clothing, loaded up on debt and rolled out pre-assembled toys that distanced children from the building experience. However, this wasn't an easy turnaround, since one of the most difficult things that Knudstorp had to do was let go of hundreds of employees to reduce overhead.

In order to make the best decision, Knudstorp went overseas to the factories and talked to each person, on a one-on-one basis, trying to understand their reality, but also using the Law of Connection. Knudstorp was effectively turning around the morale by addressing the employees' concerns on the bottom tier and letting them know that he was thinking about the future of everyone in the company and was determined to turn it around. His ability to connect with people was one of his strongest attributes as a leader. As he said, "They were asking: 'What does the future look like?' Of course, I couldn't guarantee it. But it showed that he cared for them. Being honest and transparent is important for morale." Under Knudstorp tenure, LEGO Group's yearly income has gone from a loss to drawing a notable profit and a 600% increase in revenue from 6.3 billion to 37.9 billion in 2016. In December 2016, it was announced that Knudstorp would step down as CEO of LEGO. A happy ending that ultimately ensured that our children will have the same nostalgic experience with LEGOs as we did.

As a leader, learning to motivate a follower is what defines someone. From these past examples, a leader must touch the minds as well as the hearts to motivate a following. To further increase the strength of a leader, Maxwell proposed another Law of Leadership, which he coins as the Law of Addition. This particular law falls under four axioms:

1. We add value to others when we... truly value others.

2. We add value to others when we ... make ourselves more valuable to others.

3. We add value to others when we ... know and relate to what others value.

4. We add value to others when we ... do things that God values.

Out of these four axioms, points number one and three are worth expanding upon since they are relevant to the theme of connecting with authentic leadership. Not that God or personal development are not important, but rather I would like to keep this chapter focused. With this intention, if we value others, we are more receptive to their input, leading to a psychological safe environment, but also to one that fosters feedback. To know and relate to what others value is a true testament to the Attunement aspect of authenticity defined earlier.

While the Law of Connection may seem useful at the top of a hierarchy, back in the chapter on Authentic Management, the Google Project Aristotle found that one of the top things that contributes to an effective team is psychological safety. Again, with the concept of authenticity, each level of a hierarchy has the opportunity to be authentic and connect with the people they lead, in order to create that connection, but also create that culture where people feel safe to take risks.

## Understanding the Complexity of Authentic Leadership

It is very easy to claim that transparency stemming from authentic leadership should be imperative for all companies and situations. However, there are many situations where transparency and authentic leadership should not be utilized for the sake of the company. When evaluating whether or not information should be disclosed, a good rule of thumb is looking at the worst-case scenario and, if that happens without information sharing, would that be appropriate? If yes, then proceed relentlessly.

A common dilemma surrounding transparency occurs when a company is being acquired. In fact, this example originally stemmed from my parents' company when they were on course to being acquired by another company for their data. This is a very common dilemma for founders of companies, so it is probably worth taking a closer look at. In this case, my parents were in a tight situation, since they still needed to prepare all of the data beforehand, so there was a possibility that their company would not be acquired. At the time, they had about 15 employees who would need to be let it go if the company was acquired. Taking a look at this situation, here are the best/worst cases:

From the Employee Standpoint:

| Parents tell employees | Worst Case Action | Worst Case Result |
| --- | --- | --- |
| Yes | Employees all become nervous and leave. | Company lost employees and was not acquired which ultimately leads to the company's downfall from losing employees. |
| No | Parents put together contract and lead successful acquisition. | Employees all have to be let go immediately after the transaction takes place without any pay. |

While my parents did go through with the acquisition, they were able to acknowledge the worst-case scenario and were well aware of what would take place if they made a mistake. My mother said that one of the negotiation points that they took very seriously was getting the employees hired by the larger company. Unfortunately, this was not an option because the company was only interested in the data and not in the human capital. Therefore, they settled on a transaction that involved getting at least one month of severance pay for each of the employees and amazing references to get then in the doors at other companies to reduce the damage from the changes. As a result, in the acquisition, they were able to make the best long-term decision for the company, while also being considerate of their employees. This important consideration had long time repercussions since some of these employees choose to work for my parents today.

Another example where a company would break from complete transparency is when a company is running low on funds. If an employer tells their employees about this when the situation is not as bad as it seems, employees might jump ship and avoid interacting with the company. The tricky part is when do you tell the staff that things are tough? Because of this dilemma, I suggest keeping financials more transparent earlier in the conversation than too late. What I mean by this is establishing a way that employees can understand the general direction of funds from the earliest part of their tenure. In my own company, I have the entire team aware of how much we have in our pipeline and CRM at all times. If we have a bad month, they will be the first to know.

Understanding that balance is key to developing an authentic culture: telling everyone everything would be counterproductive for the company while leaving the employees in the dark would be cruel. If the leaders of the organizations hide information and the employees find out, the trust bond breaks and needs repair. However, there are details that are worth keeping quiet in situations where a leader can mitigate the worst-case scenario. That is to say, what determines an authentic leader is their ability to navigate the waters in those crucial times.

## Tips and Tools for Making a Culture More Transparent

In relation to creating an individual authentic leader, the University of Florida wrote an organizational development paper called *Creating a Culture of Transparency*. In this research, the scholars found eight factors that leaders can deploy to create transparent cultures. Interestingly enough, when comparing to the first chapter of authenticity - alignment, attunement and vulnerability, there was immense similarity between the paper and the authenticity points.

| Attribute | Authentic Correlation |
|---|---|
| Show others that you care | Attunement |
| Be Vulnerable | Vulnerability |
| Be fiercely Honest | Vulnerability & Congruence |
| Hold the tough conversations | Vulnerability |
| Pay Attention to the mood in the office | Attunement |
| Keep your promises | Attunement |
| Be Composed | Attunement & Congruence |
| Deliver Bad News Well | Attunement & Vulnerability & Congruence |

One the flip side, there are many things that you can do to improve the surroundings to improve the workplace culture. Here are a few:

- **Town Hall Meetings**: A method mentioned before constantly, but in these meetings it is important to address the positive and negative, maybe even have a few employees present in them as well so it does not feel like the entire staff is drinking the Kool Aid of the executive team. One way of getting around this is to have a Q&A portion at all-hands where employees can submit their questions to the executive team live. The way that the executive team can answer these questions, in a non-political way, will determine how receptive the audience is.

- **Board of OKRs (Objective and Key Results Areas)**: Internally reviewing with each team what product requirements are, and what the engineering requirements are. This allows the employees of different roles to have the ability to attach a "why" to the actions that they are doing.

- **Internally Posted Goals of Teams**: One thing that I really liked is the approach that Lithium Technologies took by having each team post their goals and their progress on each one on the walls of the company. That way, as you walked by the office, you could see exactly what each team was up to.

- **Anonymous Suggestion Box**: Having one of these boxes in front of your desk, especially if you are an executive and manager. Sometimes having a physical item, like a box, is easier than sending an email to the inbox.

- **Sharing tough lessons**: Occasionally, during all-hands or team meetings, sharing tough lessons and then taking responsibility for them.
- **#General Room**: Having a general virtual room on a platform such as Slack where the water cooler talk can take place. In addition, executives can also jump into the conversation to appear more affable and relatable.

With this series of tangible actions, you will have an easier time building an authentic workplace and, on top of that, you will also understand the "why" behind different actions and their effectiveness. Unfortunately, it is very easy to write and talk about the subject but incredibly difficult to *walk the talk*. That is why you will often see many companies doing physical things that imply a transparent workplace, instead of requiring the leaders themselves to be authentically transparent. Even with writers, it is easier to sell quick-fix solutions in blog articles and with products that will miraculously improve your employee retentions by somehow helping the transparency of the workplace culture. Long fixes, like changing who you are as a person, do not sell well, nor are they easy to implement. So, they become the last place we look when attempting to solve a complex problem like transparency in a corporate workplace. It is much easier to tell the executive team that we need glass offices to fix the unhealthy culture, than turning the conversation around and telling them that they need to change.

Change, more often than not, starts at the top, but it requires those who are at the top to either take an honest look at themselves and make the necessary changes or be receptive to others' opinions about them. They have to ask themselves as leaders of the organization what they can do to capture the hearts and minds of the company. In other words, a group of inauthentic leaders cannot expect an authentic culture if they themselves do not value authenticity.

Chapter 7

# Moving Forward in the Authentic Workplace

*Piano, guitars and beanie bags. The rumors were true after all.*

**In my sanctuary,** all 6 square feet of it, the two grey walls and table were going to be my home for the next 3 months. Every weekday in a $300 chair that was probably approved by a Feng Shui consultant, I would stare into a 20-inch flat screen monitor for hours on end, remaining motionless except for my fingers. At that time, anything over that length was considered a rare treasure. In a box about 15 feet in diameter, shared with two other lucky individuals, together we would all type on our boards for hours each day. This was heaven to me. I had a place in the world and someone was paying me to occupy it. However, just outside my serenity, there was a room that I thought only existed in the rumors of Silicon Valley.

With the curiosity of a child, I soon peered into the mysterious room that was planted in the middle of the cubicle field, inside was everything that a teenager would love and so would a budding musician. It looked like a recording studio out of Nashville Tennessee mixed with a professional gaming room. There were instruments, video games and bean bags spread across the floor. Alarmingly though, and slightly nostalgic of childhood, the room was painted an obnoxious bright green and purple. Along the floor there were wires running each way under a blue rug to a massive tv that was mounted right next to the doorway I was standing in. The room not only contained the best distractions known to man, but also all of those things that I had wished my parents would buy me at Christmas during my childhood years. Was it paradise or horror? It was hard to tell, but someone thought it was a good idea.

Throughout the day, employees would walk into the office after they were playing ping pong and continue their entertainment filled afternoons and pound on a keyboard or a remote control for a video game. It did not matter the age; there were old people in there as well as young college students. My own boss at the time, Dave something, his last name escapes me at the moment, was pushing 60 and would occasionally walk into that room and begin playing video games in the middle of the day. At the time, I was 21 and I was in my first corporate software engineering internship.

For a long time, I read about Silicon Valley companies that were creating playful workplaces that seemed ridiculous, but now, I had viable proof that such a thing existed. The bean bag culture was real. However, the Silicon Valley culture was not the first place to acquire a taste for the bean bag. According to archeologists, the first bean bags were reportedly invented over 4,000 years ago by the ancient Egyptians, small round leather pouches filled with pebbles. They were used more as an act for the world's first jugglers instead of a seat of inspiration for a Mac lover. Later in history, bean bags were spotted in ancient China and among the Native Americans, and were of course used for all purposes outside of the workplace. Unsurprisingly. It wasn't until the 1960s that bean bags were first used as furniture, and the first patent was filed in 1968 as the sea urchin chair. Then someone had the great idea of throwing them into the workplace.

By introducing things such as bean bags and toys in the workplace, it is almost as though our employers want us to continue being young and not face the reality that we live in. Assuming that we are too naive to see that the longer they keep us in the office, the more likely we are to build relationships with other employees, and the stronger those relationships, the more likely we are to be retained. Though, even more immediate, if we stay longer in the office, the more we make our job the center of our lives and are able to produce more work.

Creating these kinds of environments could be likened to a cow herd being pushed through the cattle course to its inevitable fate that Mary Temple Grandin was famously known to have created back in the 90s. Simply putting toys in front of naive employees to create happiness and engagement assumes that we never look up and question why this has come to be.

But as many people know, you cannot buy your way into happiness. So why do employers assume that toys and silly things usually only kept for childhood should be brought into the workplace? Are people not intelligent enough to realize that this is not a long-term solution? And better yet, is this a part of the future? Will all workplace begin to buy toys in mass quantities hoping that creating a fun environment keep employees? Is this really what we are to look forward to in the future of the workplace?

## In The Defense of Toy Land

Before I unpack where the future of work is headed, what experts say and how this relates to authenticity, there are a few things worth pointing out about my position for avoiding work as toyland or the bean bag culture. First off, one of the largest initiatives for people in Human Resources at companies is to create a working environment that people want to be in. As Marissa Mayer, the former CEO of Yahoo, puts it: "It's about getting the best people, retaining them, nurturing a creative environment and helping to find a way to innovate." Even if that means taking part of the budget and spending it on things that people considered fun, toys, games, etc. — companies are now open to doing so.

Sooyeol Kim, a researcher from Kansas State University, discovered that "by interacting with friends or family members through a smartphone or by playing a short game, we found that employees can recover from some of their stress to refresh their minds and take a break." Thus, employees who could take breaks playing games reported that they were happier and more productive. Alina Dizik at

BBC, suggested that the best time to play games at work is during periods where employees are less productive. Hence, it is fair to say that, as long as companies focus on creating a fun working environment, bean bags and games will continue to be present in the workplace. As long as people vote for bean bags and games as fun, then the trend of the bean bag culture will continue. However, this does not mean all companies will need to add this to their working environment; it is more of an optional item that some employees will request.

## HR Innovation in the Workplace

So, bean bags will have a place in the future, fine. But, how will innovation and technology impact the future of the workplace? As much as new HR entrepreneurs continue to pitch companies, we will always see something new up and coming in the area of employee engagement and retention as well as matching new up and coming technology. Without referencing previous trends in Human Resource management, it is almost assumed that organizations have always struggled with engagement turnover and now this magical new device that a company is pitching will cure all of its problems. As Grant Cardone, four-time *New York Times* best-selling author in sales, stated: "you must be the only one who can deliver value to the customer." Essentially, in marketing you need to push your product as though it is the only solution to a particular problem. Even if it solves a problem that humans already have the ability to solve.

Here is the problem though: workplace issues such as employee engagement have been around for hundreds of years, meaning that there have been groups, tribes, that have had amazing success with engagement without having to have crazy amounts of technology at their disposal. This implies that there is a variable that existed before technology and these new tactical approaches to the workplace that become commonplace without technology. Groups in every time period have struggled without these resources and still came out successful.

What has remained consistent throughout time is human interaction and an organization's ability to lead effectively. However, that is something that does not sell well because people already have the capability to engage, lead, and manage effectively without robust help through technology. In further adding to the complexity of a simplistic solution, that means that some people are not fit in their role and should be removed from a company in order for it to survive. Simply telling an organization to fire all of its poor performing managers is not exactly what people want to hear. Usually the quick fix is what companies are looking for. A Positive ROI technology that is expected to revolutionize the workplace can gather employee feedback simply by tracking eye movement; or better yet, using Artificial Intelligence (AI) tools to monitor how well meetings are run. I mean, are people just not thinking about the impacts of having AI-run meetings? This was an actual company that no longer exists. I am not making this up, though I'd rather not say the name because I actually know the founder.

Imagine sitting through another boring meeting that now has an agenda that was precompiled by an AI machine and was being monitored by a little black device in the middle of the room. If someone spoke too long, the device would interrupt, let them know they are getting off track, then ask for someone else to speak. I assure you, that device would be fired faster than anything you ever seen. Now keep in mind, I am very much for innovation and new ideas in the workplace, even though the past few pages make it seem like I am very against it. The reason why I take this stance is because that I believe we truly undervalue our own intrinsic ability to connect with one other and build a working environment that is desirable to be in.

We have an immense amount of dominant ability that resides in each and every one of us, but we often focus externally on the world, so that we never come into contact with our own ability to connect with each other. In conclusion, HR technology will continue to become prevalent in the space of the workplace, but it will not be able to undercut the value of human interaction and connection. Outside of HR Technology, here are a couple of other trends that will be impacting the workplace in the up and coming years:

## Globalization

As a political hot topic in the presidency of Bill Clinton, globalization is still becoming more and more impactful. Jack Ma, CEO of the Chinese e-commerce company Alibaba, said globalization, and the advances it is bringing, should be embraced, stating that in the past 30 years, globalization benefited about 6 percent of businesses. In the next 30 years, he said the data shows "at least 60 percent of the small business will be global, will benefit from the globalization."

Depending on your viewpoint, globalization could be a positive or negative change.

What this means on more of a micro level is that teams in companies will not hail from the same territory, or rather, the ability to grow a company will be substantially easier. Because every company will have the ability for global reach through technology and build their teams internationally, with technology enabling employees to work from all over the world. According to the Zinc survey, IDC expects mobile workers will account for nearly three-quarters of the U.S. workforce by 2020. At first, this was just for telemarketers, but now it is bleeding into just about every job position where technology allows. Doctors performing diagnoses remotely, nurses taking care of patients through machines, and executives closing multimillion-dollar deals through video. "The remote workforce is growing at an astonishing rate … and it'll be up to employers to keep up with the changing needs of their employees," said Stacey Epstein, CEO of Zinc. "One of the easiest adjustments management can make is to implement a companywide set of communication standards that simplifies the process for their workers so they're not switching between email, SMS and a slew of apps not secure enough for the enterprise." In the long run, you should expect to see more globalization on the horizon of the workplace.

## Virtual/Augmented Reality

Workplaces can expand beyond physical boundaries to connect employees and customers using virtual reality. Employees may connect with each other in a virtual meeting space, rather than over a conference call. Eventually, this will allow for non-verbal communication, interactive presentations, or virtual collaboration by remote employees as if they were in the office together. This use case for VR is anticipated and highly valued. According to Dell's Future Workforce study,[31] 67 percent of millennials believe it is important to use virtual reality in meetings and product development.

Let's dive a bit deeper into the evolution of Virtual/Augmented Reality. In a summary from NewGenApps, in 1968, the first VR headset was created; in 1990, the term Augmented Reality was coined; in 1994, the first theater production of augmented reality was released; in 2009, ARToolKit a free open source code base was published giving public access to underlying code; in 2017, Android and iOS published AR Cores in their hardware so that their devices could support AR experiences. With these recent trends, Augmented Reality is no longer a commercial idea but now a consumer product that is increasing in its development.

On the robotics side, Double Robotics Double came out a few years ago with robots that roll through the office with only a wheel and a long pole for an iPad. The end goal is to bring remote employees into the workplace. It is as though the remote worker is able to walk the office, as if they are there and interact with other employees. I recall seeing this back in 2014 when they first came out when a floating iPad with someone's face on it was right next to my desk.

---

31   https://www.dellemc.com/en-us/workforce-solutions/purposedrivendesigns.htm#section=next-decade

In the previous section, as remote employees increase, there will be an increased need for human connection, so having augmented reality to allow employees to connect with one another will be a big shift. Hence, one can suspect to see an increase in augmented reality in the workplace to help with the aspects of communicating and connecting with intercontinental teams.

## The Gig Economy

John McAfee, CEO of McAfee software, described the gig economy as" "empowerment. This new business paradigm empowers individuals to better shape their own destiny and leverage their existing assets to their benefit."

For those of you who are not as familiar with this buzzword, the gig economy is made up of three main components: independent workers paid by the gig (*i.e.*, a task or a project) as opposed to those workers who receive a salary or hourly wage; consumers who need a specific service, for example, a ride to their next destination, or a particular item delivered; and the companies that connect the worker to the consumer in a direct manner, including app-based technology platforms. Companies such as Uber, Airbnb, Lyft, Etsy or TaskRabbit act as the medium through which the worker is connected to – and ultimately paid by – the consumer. These companies make it easier for workers to find a quick, temporary job (*i.e.*, a gig), which can include any kind of work, from a musical performance to fixing a leaky faucet. One of the main differences between a gig and traditional work arrangements, however, is that a gig is a temporary work engagement, and the worker is paid only for that specific job.

While this does sound promising, having worked with companies that are effectively running companies on a gig economy basis, they struggle to find repeat work and employees who will stay using their business. The gig economy marks a rise of entrepreneurship while it puts pressure on the general public to produce small amounts of work in incremental bits, rather than having a long stream of work production. My hypothesis is that we will see growth of the gig economy as work can be more broken down into tasks that don't involve full time employees.

## Trends and Their Toll on Authenticity

While these trends sound fascinating and exciting, it also means that the world will take some time to adapt to the worldwide changes. However, that is the structure of the way the world works. Globalization is how teams will be formed, putting pressure and concern on how remote teams communicate and are managed. Virtual reality is the medium for experience other people. The gig economy is the way that people are opting to work differently. It is not how people actually relate to one another within those systems, which means authenticity will continue as we live in the world that is continually being separated.

Now that we have covered authenticity intensively, we can now observe how these trends play a role in the increased need for authenticity.

Let's take a look at the first one, globalization. With the world becoming more and more connected every day, cultures are becoming melded and viewpoints are shared. However, there is quite a lot of friction that will develop when different teams from different countries work together. Imagine as your organization become more acquainted with working with other teams across the world on similar projects, how communication is very difficult because of culture and language barriers. Most likely there will be miscommunications and work ethic expectation clashes between the different teams, as though it was a car engine with pistons that were all firing at different times.

When a problem or miscommunication arises, which they inevitably do in work teams, the ability to think empathetically and address the situation critically remains of paramount importance in order to keep the team together. Fortunately, humans speak a universal language of emotion and authenticity is the perfect channel to resonate. Given this obstacle, understanding is the first thing that people need to do.

The second is virtual reality. Here, people are looking to make reality more exciting by adding technology to the mix. With this new experience, people will be able to learn more and do more work at a distance. However, human connection is still an essential property and being able to fulfill that lost sense is important. In a sense, it does bring us closer together where we can have a virtual reality meeting where everyone shows up as an avatar, but there is still the issue of being in the presence of another human being. Addressing the Congruence is extremely important in addressing the shift to a more Virtual Reality-based environment.

Lastly, the gig economy. In 2018, I was consulting for a company that could be the considered the Uber for babysitters where their platform would literally line up its babysitters with work repeatedly with the babysitters not having to do any marketing. On the surface this seems like the dream for a college student: sit in a dorm, download the app, and be given work. However, there was a substantial flaw in this design, there was no emotion, no sense of community, so engagement was not there. Which meant a lot of sitters left the platform and joined places like Starbucks, where they would be interacting with coworkers on a day-to-day basis. While not true for all people who join the gig economy, there is an extreme issue where it is very lonely. People crave connection. So, what was the proposed solution?

We devised a strategy that involve teams that helped increase engagement where the team leaders would be sitters themselves and would be able to foster a community of sitters, where each person felt like they belonged. However, in order for that to happen, the team leader needed to have an ability to lead and connect, in other words, be authentic. Without being authentic, sitters would simply leave and go somewhere else. Having a gig economy is creative but it misses an important part of human connection that is universally desired.

## The Movement Towards An Authentic Workplace

One of the biggest goals I had in writing this book is to help people realize that the power of being authentic could dramatically help one lead, manage and retain employees. Hence, making enormous change in their lives without spending thousands of dollars. However, through my observations of the changing world in which we live in, I learned that as we become more connected through technology, we simultaneously become more disconnected. In an odd way, as we close the gap between each other by creating technology in order to communicate across seas, we remove the curiosity of having to cross the sea itself.

In addition, the increasing dependency on quick solutions to complex problems that has been plaguing groups for hundreds of years remains, such as an app to track feedback or a few tricks in building rapport with employees. We become more reliant on technology as an easy fix for complex solutions that might not be as simple as swiping left and right. My hope is that, instead of people looking for an external solution for their problems in the workplace, they would look within and understand that many of the problems that exist in the workplace can be resolved with an ability that they already have and produce a massive positive change.

For authenticity is not one-size-fits-all type of solution, for it's one complex tool to a complex puzzle. If there was a formulaic way to increase engagement or create the ideal culture, all companies would be doing it, because no debate would be necessary. Looking back, remember that authenticity is not a matter of just being yourself as mainstream media suggests. Rather, in this book I argue it's a tri-fold process: Congruence, Vulnerability and Attunement.

Which in itself, is a very challenging task. All three aspects of finding who you are, empathetically understanding your audience, and learning how to evoke emotion with language are tough. It is a journey to continuously find out who one is, and enhance your ability to understand the world, the ability to be authentic will increase in unison. I hope there will be a day where people will stop looking outside themselves for the answers to life's complex problems and instead, look within.

With that said, I will like to tell you a short story that had a dramatic impact on my life and my understanding of the necessity there is for human connection and being authentic with one another.

It seems pretty silly to believe that 100 years from now, the big change will be basically people needing to be authentic with one another? Sure, there will be many advancements in the workplace, but that vision does not appear innovative or trendy enough to sell as a story to a media outlet like *Wired* or *Forbes*. Do people really think that we will eventually have enough technology to completely remove people from the system of connection? Hundreds of dystopias have been written on this very subject where people were working in isolation and inevitably never interacted with one another because they had all of the technology that they needed to exist. One of my favorite future dystopias was written by E.M. Forster, titled *The Machine Stops,* which shows a very possible reality of a world relying too heavily on technology.

## The Machine Stops

In this short story dystopia, humans have moved below the Earth's surface, and all live in a firma where their every need is met, and every act controlled by "the machine." This machine is the same type of machine that we have today; think of Nest or a house that will do everything for you. Each person living underground individually lives in their own honeycomb shaped room where the machine is able to assist whatever comes about. Long pipes and tubes outside of the room transport whatever is needed in between rooms: medicine, clothing, accessories, you name it, it's shipped. The creators of the machine were long deceased, and the people who currently operate it don't have a clear understanding of all of the parts. Consequently the machine runs itself at that point in time.

During the early point of the story, Forster mentions a few things worth noting about how one of people's primary purposes is to share ideas with one another. No one works or does any hard labor, people do not touch since that is considered primitive and exploration is considered primitive. Occasionally, people do travel to the surface of the planet, move around the planet in a speedy fashion, but they rarely ever look out the windows, because, according to their paradigm, there are new ideas outside. If anyone is to walk around on the surface, they will need to wear special equipment to move around because the air is toxic.

After many years living under the Earth's surface, humans ultimately start to worship the machine since, in a convoluted sense, it is response for all of their interactions and care. Oddly, all new thoughts and human interaction is shunned by the machine as it is able to accommodate almost every need imaginable. Characters in the book are described as having a heavenly feeling where they are able to let go to everything when they are in the arms of the machine.

This story is centered around Vashti and her son, Kuno, as they struggle in the world of separation to form a meaningful relationship. Kuno has a dream of exploring the world outside of his room and actively expresses disgust for the machine throughout the beginning of the book. Early in the story, Kuno summons his mother Vashti to visit him because he has urgent news. His mother, living on the other side of the planet, begrudgingly takes the next plane over to her son's place, as to her, it would be much easier to do a screen call to communicate instead of traveling halfway across the planet. Kuno proclaims this to Vashti to warn her after he has made it to the Earth's surface, showing that the reliance on technology ended up leading to a corrupt society that never had a chance of succeeding.

Vashti does not take her son's discoveries seriously and continues on with her life as though they never met. In the act of exploration, her son, Kuno, was threatened with homelessness due to his behavior of exploring the Earth's surface. Homelessness essentially meant death. Fortunately, he was not executed but instead transported to a different part of the world.

Sometime later, Vashti gets a message from Kuno that the machine is coming to an end soon. Skeptical, she continues on with her monotony until the power was suddenly cut off from her room. No buttons, screens, or tools work. She was left in complete darkness. Fortunately, she was able to open the door to escape her room, as it worked through a crank and not the Machine and walked outside to see what happened to the world of the machine.

Outside of Vashti's room, the entire underworld was in complete chaos as everyone else was just as disoriented as Vashti. Eventually, fires break out and people start to run in panic in every direction imaginable. Vashti, amidst the chaos, is left in pitch blackness. The only thing she knows to do is to cry for help. Kuno, serendipitously found his mother in these final hours and they comforted each other. For the first time in the story, they held one another and expressed the affection and died in each other's arms.

## Bringing It Home

*The Machine Stops* argues that an over-reliance on technology will end up leading to a society that has no chance of survival. With technology being a paramount part of the world that they live in, they subsequently use the Machine for parts of their lives that normally calls for human connection. Unfortunately, from this continuous use, the machine becomes a religion and eventually God to some degree to the people.

That is how Forster fabricates an environment where people lived their lives in isolation because technology allowed humans to avoid interaction. Even though humans created the machine they worship, the machine itself has a power that can be unmatched and makes it invincible. Technology ended up replacing any other authority figures for this society, including religious figures such as gods or kings. It became the savior and soul caregiver in a land where isolation was commonplace. In a twisted sense, it sounds very similar to the anthropological adjustments that technology is having on the way we relate to one another.

While this short story was not focused on technology and the drawbacks for civilization, it serves as an example to note what happens as our tendencies to value our human attributes like authenticity are neglected. As we began to delegate multiple human activities and replace them with external uses such as technology, we slowly drain our society of what it means to be human. By replacing our working environments with models and processes that increase effectiveness, we consequently remove our need for being human, separating ourselves further and further from each other even though we continue to have a deep craving for intimacy. There is no replacement for the human connection, no matter how advanced our world is. Humans are humans not machines, which means if you want to attract people to your company, manage them effectively, or lead them, a human touch is needed.

Throughout hundreds of stories written about the future, when we remove this connection and are able to delegate it to some kind of technology, we find ourselves looking in a well of emptiness for what happened to be a shadow of the world and its obsolete connection. An inhuman void that scares back expressionless. We are already seeing the paradoxical effects of social media with its excessive amount of time spent on these platforms leading to depression and isolation. It is fair to conclude that this emptiness will only continue to grow as we ignore the fact that we ultimately are human and want connection. We must remember that we are the creators of the place that we call work, which means that we also have the ability to shape it into a structure that is mutually beneficial. You already have the innate ability to be authentic; in other words, you already have everything you need to succeed in the workplace.

By and large, being authentic is one of the most difficult things to do in this world. One must learn to look inside and understand who they are as a person, become attuned with someone else's reality and lastly, be emotionally vulnerable. There is much respect due a person who is able to evoke this kind of character in the workplace, because with the ever-changing circumstances in which we live, we will continuously be facing a battle of human interaction and optimization.

# About the Author

Jeffery Butler was born in 1991 in a suburban town in Silicon Valley, California. He attended high school near Google headquarters in Mountain View. At 17, he was having a relatively normal high school experience until he was diagnosed with a potentially fatal form of depression. This event motivated him to study psychology in hopes of surviving his disorder.

During his journey of survival, he managed to graduate high school, attended UC Berkeley as an athlete and later finish college with a degree in Computer Science in 2014. He continued to struggle with depression until he met a doctor who helped him create the breakthrough of a lifetime. After creating this breakthrough, he shifted his focus to his career as a software engineer.

Two years later at 25, he returned to his roots of psychology and began to share his findings with others. Since then, he has spoken at *Fortune* 500 companies, such as Google, Amazon, conferences such as TEDx, to thousands of students nationwide at high schools and appeared on radio and TV. He currently resides in Berkeley, California where he continues his mission of helping others become the person they desire to be.

If you are interested in hiring Jeff to speak at your event, please go to his website: jeffjbutler.com or you can email him personally at jeff@jeffjbutler.com.

www.ingramcontent.com/pod-product-compliance
Lightning Source LLC
Chambersburg PA
CBHW071020240526
45469CB00006BD/2011